How the Investment Business Really Works

by

Ken Kaszak

a
valuekaszak
book

Pittsburgh • San Ysidro • Las Tunas

Library of Congress Control Number: 2002106299

Kaszak, Kenneth
How the Investment Business Really Works
ISBN 0-9720870-0-1

valuekaszak
p.o. box 4278
pittsburgh, pa 15203
valuekaszak@yahoo.com

Third Printing
Printed in the United States of America

INTRODUCTION

In the autumn of 1997 I was living in a rented townhouse in the Whitehall section of Pittsburgh. Since entering the investment business a few years earlier, I had written various articles about the mechanics of the investment business and the proper way to structure an investment portfolio. I had also begun to develop a reputation of teaching clients and potential clients the true workings of the investment industry.

I decided to link the articles together with some freshly written essays and put them into a booklet format. I wanted to walk the reader through a step-by-step approach to the business by providing only the information that was relevant and showing how those items were interrelated.

I wrote the essays on my Smith-Corona word processor at my dining room table. John Mellencamp's *"Mr. Happy-Go-Lucky"* played over and over on my CD player. When I think about that writing project, I think about John Cougar Mellencamp.

The booklet ended up 35 pages in length. I would take the original to Kinko's and have them print a cover on blue card stock *(BC9 Lunar Blue)* and bind a cover *(velo binding)* onto the pages. The booklets were printed up 2 or 3 at a time and I would give them to potential clients.

The booklets served their purpose. They became an efficient teaching tool and helped me acquire more clients. Many people who became clients probably didn't read the material but figured I knew what I was doing because I had put the booklet together. It was always a thought of mine to one day expand that booklet into a book. And that is what you are about to read.

Because I don't want to lose the power of those 35 pages and what they meant to me, I am going to introduce this book with the same introductory letter that prefaced that previous work. Here it is:

Dear Investor:

I am a fan of thought-provoking quotes. One of my favorite quotes is this one:

The only thing constant is change.

While a certain amount of change and evolution is always present in every industry, the investment business is currently undergoing a tremendous amount of change. This change is being fueled by increased competition, new competitors and the explosion of investment-related information and resources available to the public.

But not all of that information has value to it. Not all of what you hear from investment sales people, financial planners, "media brokers" and see in print is being used to educate you. As with any sales effort, there is hype and scam and noise mixed in with the relevant data. And a large part of what you hear is actually being used to divert you from what you need to know to make proper and prudent investment decisions.

And that's where I come in.

I am an economist by training, an investment banker by profession and a CPA-certified instructor. I am a specialist in two things: IRS Code Section 42 Tax Credits (which provide Federal Tax Credits in return for investments in affordable housing) and teaching people how the investment business really works.

I am building my reputation by teaching clients the history and mechanics of the capital markets and the importance of proper asset allocation, low management fees, and low portfolio turnover rates. Most brokers do what they need to do to gain the trust of clients. What I do is give clients the knowledge they need in order to trust themselves.

What you are about to read is a collection of articles and essays about the investment business. These articles are the result of my diverse, unique and illuminating journey through the business. Once you read and digest these articles you will know a majority of what the average financial salesperson knows. More important: you will put yourself in the best position possible when dealing with investment matters and people in the business.

I know that my experiences and insight will become of value to you.

Kenneth Kaszak
Registered Representative
October 1997

As proof that the quote about change holds true, since I wrote that letter the number of people trying to acquire your investment dollars has increased, the marketing and advertising effort of the industry has been stepped up and the amount of conflicting information being thrown at you has exploded. Because of the increase in the importance of 401(k) plans, Roth IRAs, Education IRAs and other savings plans that shift the responsibility away from your employer and put it on you, it has become even more important that you become financially competent. This book will give you the knowledge and confidence you will need to make those investment decisions.

The original title of my booklet was **"How the Investment Business Really Works...*and how it should work.* "** I dropped the tag line, but once you read this book you will know how the business should work.

Part One provides some background information on myself and shares the story of how I became involved in the investment business. Part Two is the heart and soul of this book. It contains ten interrelated sections. Each section serves as a prerequisite for the next. Part Three is a collection of essays designed to give you insight into the personalities involved in the business and why your best interest usually takes a backseat to theirs. For reasons you will understand when you finish this book, outlining and writing Part Three was a labor of love.

Ken Kaszak
August 2002

PART

ONE

The only joy in the
world is to begin.

— Cesare Pavese (Italian writer;1908-1950)

There are many places where this story can begin. Since I'm a believer that every part of a person's past is connected to every part of his or her present and future, I will begin by providing you with information from my own beginnings. This part of my life shaped my work ethic, my sensitivity, the way I treat people and gave me my ambition and my desire to create, achieve and accomplish.

My childhood could have been a series of Norman Rockwell paintings. I grew up in a middle-class neighborhood in the South Hills of Pittsburgh. My parents' romance and marriage is worthy of a book of its own. My father, son of Polish immigrants, married my mother, the Serbian daughter of pool room operators (and part-time bookies) even though people of Serbian and Polish descent did their best to keep their children away from each other. My father played on a Catholic League state basketball championship team in high school and was the 500,000th person drafted into the Korean War *(a chance occurrence that made him the subject of articles in local and national newspapers, a USO trip to Japan and a dinner date with the actress Patricia Neal...right before he was sent to the front lines and placed in a foxhole)*. Although he was chased away from the pool hall by my grandfather-to-be on his first attempt to take my mother on a date, he persisted and married a beautiful, sensitive girl who grew into a beautiful sensitive mother of three boys. Persistence is a trait I acquired from my parents and it is also my adopted middle name. My parents are both deceased but live through me and my brothers not only in the way we look and act, but in the way we work, the way we play and the way we treat people.

My family lived in a comfortable three-bedroom house located on a cul-de-sac. The backyard of our house sat atop Elm Leaf Park, and there were two baseball fields within walking distance. We walked to school up until the eighth grade. Except for the days my mother was working as a Kelly Girl, we were able to come home for lunch. I have a strong memory of standing next to one or both of my brothers as my mother combed our hair before sending us back to school after making us cinnamon French Toast.

My father spray painted bases in the cul-de-sac, and we played various forms of baseball and kickball along with touch football in the street. Basketball hoops were scattered throughout the neighborhood. Elm Leaf Park, with its various trails, hills, valleys and dense brush, was the sight of numerous day long hikes, battles with imaginary Indians and Nazi soldiers and tree house developments. In the winter, the local fire company flooded the basketball court in the park and turned it into an ice skating rink. There were days when I was in the 5th and 6th grades where I would wake up early, get dressed and walk down the path behind our house to the part-time ice rink. Ice skating at 6:30 in the morning before going to school is a memory I wish everyone could share.

My father would drive my brothers and me to the Carnegie Library on a regular basis. We would run up the steps into the building and go straight to the children's reading room. The books we checked out on sports, history and space exploration gave us a solid foundation of knowledge in a variety of subjects. The voracious reading habit my parents instilled in me remains one of the best gifts they ever gave to me.

My high school career was shaped by a serious back injury I suffered while playing tight end and linebacker on the tenth grade football team. I had a back operation at the beginning of my junior year and was tutored at home for five months. I spent most of my time reading novels and watching classic black & white movies into the early morning hours. When I returned to school for my senior year, the same drive and energy I had applied to playing sports was channeled to the theater arts program. I adopted the persona of a hungry, angry young actor. I wore the same blue jeans, T-shirt and imitation leather jacket almost every day and drove my Honda 175 motorcycle as if it was the biggest Harley in town. I can't remember much about the class schedule my senior year except for the fact my last two classes were Theater Arts and Advanced Placement English. No matter if I cut every other class or slept through them, I made sure I was in the school and ready to go for those last two classes. I was an excellent and motivated acting student. In addition to having the lead in my senior class play, I also acted in local stage productions and had part-time jobs at a film lab and a public TV station.

After graduating from high school I turned down a suggestion from my drama teacher to try out for the prestigious Carnegie Mellon drama school. I also turned down a non-paying job as an apprentice at a summer stock theater in Connecticut to go to work. My plan was to save enough money to move to New York and attend the Stella Adler Drama School, the same school Marlon Brando attended. I got two jobs: at a Texaco station and at a warehouse. I worked 60 hours a week and tried to save money. I can't describe the difficulty in saving money when you are making less than $3.00 per hour.

Shortly after my 19th birthday, I withdrew the money I had in my bank account (including the money I received from selling my motorcycle) and boarded a Greyhound bus to New York City. I got a room at a transient hotel known as The Diplomat in Times Square and tried to establish myself in the city. I turned in my application at the drama school and put in job applications at gas stations in the neighborhood around The Diplomat. Two weeks after I arrived in New York I realized that I didn't have the two things I needed to be in New York: enough money to stay in the city and the self-confidence in my physical appearance required to become an actor. I was never enamored with the way I looked. I was about 6 foot tall, weighed 165 pounds, had broken my nose at a football practice and was a regular user of

Clearasil. I wore my hair straight back because I wanted to spend the least amount of time looking in the mirror each morning. Everywhere I went in the area around The Diplomat I saw good-looking young men whom I assumed to be actors working in the restaurants, bars and stores and walking the streets. They had the self-confidence and the financial ability to stay in the city. The city that was too big for me was not too big for them. They obviously wanted to be actors more intensely than I did. After my brief two-week run in the Big Apple, I spent my last Sunday night at Lem's, the cafeteria-style steak restaurant in Times Square. The next day I would be going back to the bus station and buying another one-way ticket. As I chowed down on my thick steak, baked potato, garlic bread and washed it down with an ice cold Molson in preparation of returning to Pittsburgh, I wondered what endeavor I was going to get involved in next. To this day, I have never learned if my application to the Stella Adler school was accepted.

Exactly two weeks to the day after I returned to Pittsburgh, I was hired as a laborer by a company that installed built-in swimming pools. I had limited experience working with tools and no aptitude for construction but jumped at the chance for employment. I was put on a crew that would arrive at a backyard after our backhoe operator had opened up a large hole. It was our job to mold that hole into a 16' X 32' swimming pool complete with sloped walls, a shallow end, a deep end, concrete sidewalks, a heater, filter, step ladders and various other amenities.

I quickly grew to love this job. I loved working with the dirt, the sand, the mud and the concrete. I loved pulling my work boots on each morning, driving around in trucks and smoking Marlboros. It was hard, physical work, but I didn't mind. Working with my body took me away from all the self-imposed deep thought and self-doubt I had put myself through. My acting aspirations quickly went behind me. I put on a few pounds of upper body weight from the physical labor and got a great tan. My boots, tight fitting jeans and white muscle T-shirt gave me a sense of self-confidence as I arrived on a job site or entered a fast food restaurant on a lunch break.

The job also provided me with something else: a sense of achievement and fulfillment when we finished a job. Two weeks after arriving at a site, given only a crudely dug hole to work with and our tools and equipment, we would leave behind a complete swimming pool with a perfectly shaped deep end, tight fitting liner, freshly poured concrete and various extra features. The families we worked for and their neighbors were always excited to see our progress and final finish. There was a great sense of accomplishment when each pool was finished. And I liked that feeling.

One of the employees of the company had ambitions of building houses. He was the son of one of the owners of the company and his first name was Joe. He was talented in the unique combined fields of construction and poetry. We got along well and would talk about poetry, home building, and girls on the truck rides to job sites.

Joe told me that the local Community College campus, less than one mile from the offices of the pool company, offered a class titled "Construction Methods I" in the fall semester. Some of the employees of the company took a few night classes during the fall semester and then loaded up on more classes during the spring semester while collecting unemployment and waiting for the start of the next pool season. I was convinced by Joe and the other workers to take the construction class at Community College. The idea of building houses in the future appealed to me. I remember thinking there would be something fulfilling, passionate and idealistic about building houses and creating the space where people lived and raised their families.

I remember a strange feeling as I made the short trip to the campus. I had been so opposed to ever attending college that I was voted "Least Likely to Attend College" by my high school classmates. For the grand price of $19.00 per credit, I signed up for the construction class. I also enrolled in English I and, looking for a class that was available on Thursday evening, I signed up for a class titled Economics I.

I remember almost nothing about the Construction Methods class. My talent working with tools remains extremely limited. The English class was of note because I was selected to read two poems in front of the class and because we had the final exam in the backroom of a local bar. But the class that did have a positive impact on me was the class in economics.

Before signing up for the class I knew that the subject had something to do with business, but I had no idea to what extent. Even in this introductory class, I realized that the subject of economics touched upon each aspect of the business world. Sitting in the back of Mr. Crocker's classroom, I could see how the study of economics took the student on a journey through the fields of accounting, finance, interest rate theory, international business, marketing, advertising and the impact of governmental policy on the business world. I saw the common thread. I came to each class (unlike high school, I would never dream of cutting a class I was paying $19.00 per credit for) and took notes. While my fellow Community College students thought the class was dull and the various charts and graphs pointless and hard to tie into any relevant meaning, I found the class insightful and challenging. I studied each chapter and reviewed my class notes in advance of each test.

Although I did all of this, my test-taking ability did not match my enthusiasm for the subject. To the best of my recollection, I got a "C" for the class, but that grade was fine with me. I was motivated by and interested in the subject of economics. I had found my next challenge. The motivation I had for economics was different than the motivation I had for sports and much different than the passion I had for acting. But the subject provided me with a sense of direction and curiosity. And that was exactly what I needed at that point in my life.

Ideas are one thing.
And what happens is another.

— John Cage (American Composer;1902-1992)

I got laid off from the swimming pool company in November and started collecting unemployment checks. I had made enough money building pools to buy a used car and to expand my wardrobe from the jeans and T-shirts I had been wearing since high school. Because I would be collecting unemployment through the winter I decided to take a total of 20 credits in both day and evening school at Community College. I remember that time well: I was 19 years old, had a few bucks in my pocket, some nice clothes, a nice car and I was living in the basement of my parents' house. When I was nineteen, it was a very good year.

Because my math skills were poor I enrolled in a basic math class. I also took a literature class, another class in economics and other classes that were forgotten long ago. I also started to read books on the subject of economics and books about well known economists. One of my brothers had given me books on the subject for Christmas and my interest in the subject exploded. Instead of reading the works of playwrights like Tennessee Williams, Arthur Miller and David Mamet as I did when studying acting, I found myself reading the works of economists like Milton Friedman, Adam Smith and John Kenneth Galbraith.

I enjoyed the classes and the social life of Community College but always referred to myself as a construction worker first and a student second. However, that was about to change because of two separate but related items.

Midway through the semester I learned I was eligible to apply for a scholarship from the state's Bureau of Vocational Rehabilitation because of my high school back injury. I also found myself on the campus of Duquesne University one night after giving a girl a ride home from a party. I liked the look of the campus enough to return a few days later for a closer look. It was a warm sunny day late in the winter when I returned, and the campus looked even better than at night. I found myself walking down the area in the middle of the campus known as Academic Walk. The sun was shining off the buildings, the students were walking back and forth between classes, and spring fever was in the air. If you were to make a movie about college life, this part of Duquesne University would be a perfect setting. I also ran into a friend who played on the same Pony League team as me and who had graduated from high school with me. He had enrolled at Duquesne right after high school and had nothing but good things to say about life at this college. I concluded my trip with a walk along Bluff Street and was impressed with the view of the city's South Side and the Monongahela River.

I filled out my BVR scholarship application and submitted it in late March. In early April I made a trip to the swimming pool company to find out when I was going to be called back to work. At the time my plan was to work through the summer and fall and take night classes until I got laid off again. However, when I sat down with the owner of the pool company, I received some bad news. He had found out about my back operation and was afraid of me getting injured at work. Although I was physically able to do the grueling work and had proven myself, the risk of an injury and higher Worker's Compensation costs was too great for the owner. We shook hands and parted on good terms, but I found myself out of a job I liked.

I have always been a believer in omens. I took this series of events as an omen. In addition to enrolling in summer school at Community College, I applied for a transfer to Duquesne University. I was still collecting my $120.00 each week from unemployment insurance and would be doing so until late in the year. When summer school ended, I went straight into the fall semester.

Early in the fall I received notice that I was accepted at Duquesne University. I also learned that the Bureau of Vocational Rehabilitation would provide me with a scholarship each semester I remained academically eligible. The tuition cost at Duquesne was still out of my reach. I applied for and received both a grant and a student loan. Late in the fall semester at Community College, it dawned on me. Here I was: a person who left high school with no intention of going to college, a person who never took the SATs or ACTs, a person whose class rank was 777 out of a class of 971, about to enter a highly regarded, academically challenging private university. I was excited but also a little concerned about my ability to do the work.

My concerns were justified. The difference between Community College and Duquesne University was not just like night and day. It was a total eclipse. Getting used to the campus and the increased number of students was difficult for me. And that was the easy part of my transition.

The classwork at Duquesne was much more difficult than at Community College. Even though the picturesque Academic Walk was one of the motivating factors for me to come to this school, I never got to see it my first semester. All of my classes were in the business school on the outskirts of campus. My routine was such that I would park my car in the South Side, take a bus into town and make the five minute walk to Rockwell Hall. I would arrive in the building right before my first class, attend my classes, and leave the building right after the last class. I would walk back into town, bus back to my car and drive home and attempt to digest the material presented in class that day.

That winter happened to be an extremely cold winter and the campus of Duquesne University, because of its location, is one of the coldest places in Pittsburgh during January and February. The wind whipping off the river, across Bluff Street and around the brick and concrete buildings, is brutal.

The coldness of that winter could not match the coldness of the professor who taught my first class in economics. This gentleman was rumored to have been a member of John Kennedy's Council of Economic Advisors and he did consulting work for various publishing companies. When he passed out the first test of the semester, it was so thick it looked like the phone book for a small town. The test consisted of essay questions and detailed analytical questions. That was fine with me. I took the test with incredible confidence. I was prepared, well rested and had studied each day during the week before the test instead of cramming the night before.

When the professor returned the test the next class he paused in front of my desk before handing back my test. He told me that he wanted to see me in his office before the end of the day. For one brief moment I thought he wanted to tell me I had the makings of a brilliant economist and to compliment me on receiving the highest grade he had ever given in his class. As he continued to the next student I looked at my grade. It was shocking to see a "D-." To add insult to injury, he had used a thick red marker on the paper. I didn't feel bad that I performed poorly on a test;I felt bad that I performed poorly on a test in economics.

After my classes were over I went to see him. He was smoking a pipe and his desk was covered with papers. You couldn't see the desktop through the mountain of papers. His office walls were adorned with bookcases from floor to ceiling. I remember scanning the titles and feeling jealous that he had read the greatest books on economics ever written. My scanning stopped when he asked me where I had transferred from. When I proudly said "Community College," he asked me to give some consideration to going back there.

This teacher was not the only member of Duquesne University who thought I should return to the Community College campus. I struggled through my first semester and ended up with a grade point average of 1.6. I received a letter from the Academic Advisors office telling me I was being placed on academic probation for the rest of my time at Duquesne. The letter also suggested I take some time away from the college and consider whether or not I would be able to do the classwork required at Duquesne.

There were two things that happened in a short period of time that are instrumental to this story. If these things hadn't happened in the order they did, this book would have no reason to be written.

Due to my abysmal 1.6 average, I had put my BVR scholarship in danger. I contacted another college in town and started exploring the process of transferring. I went to the college and met with an admissions officer. I told him about my situation at Duquesne and my troubles in the classroom. He told me that his college offered the same degree that Duquesne did, that the class work was not as difficult, and the tuition cost far less. Boy, all of that sounded good to me. I left his office with every intention of transferring.

When I reached the street I had an epiphany. My revelation was that the decision to transfer out of Duquesne was a much more important decision than moving from one college to another. The implications were much deeper. If I transferred and graduated from the other school, I would always look at my diploma as tarnished. What good would a diploma be if it was obtained in a backdoor manner? I was facing a challenge and preparing to back down without putting up any resistance. I had given up my acting ambition too easily, and if I backed down from this endeavor, quitting may have gotten too easy for me. I pride myself on my persistence now, but back then I didn't have that reputation. I had walked away from challenges from time to time. I didn't want people to refer to me as quitter, and I didn't want to think of myself as one.

As I stood outside of the admissions office and looked up to the sky, I knew what I had to do. In spite of what my economics professor had said to me, in spite of the letter I had received from the Academic Advisors office suggesting I might not be able to handle the classwork at Duquesne, I had to go back if I wanted to go forward. I had to go back to that school and fight the good fight.

The second thing that happened is that I got a summer job at a beer distributor delivering cases and barrels of beer to bars and restaurants in the Pittsburgh area. Eight hours a day, six days a week for the grand total of $140.00 per week, I rode around my city supplying the owners of shot and beer bars and fine dining establishments alike with their beer supply. This seems like it would be a great job to have and for the first three days it was. I worked with a fellow only a few years older than me who had made some money booking bands into local night clubs before he discovered the allure of drinking large amounts of gin. I got to wear my work boots again, and it was nice being away from the classes at Duquesne riding around the streets of Pittsburgh. The one fringe benefit of the job, a free beer at every stop, enabled us to get a buzz early in the morning and keep it going all day. My nights were occupied with more beer drinking and a little softball thrown in for variety.

But that job grew tired quickly. It was hard, physically demanding work and some of the tiny cellars and gang planks we had to deal with were dangerous. A half-barrel of beer weighs 173 pounds, and I weighed less than that. I found myself carrying kegs up and down rickety cellar steps and stacking them three high in basement coolers. The people I worked with, interesting characters at first, turned out to be problem drinkers and people whose futures were getting behind them in a hurry. For the most part they were on the downbound train and looking to pick up as many passengers as possible. The smell of stale beer became such an identifying part of the job that I can still smell spilled beer in the basement of a bar if I'm walking by the front door.

Why was this job an important factor in my life? Because less than one month into my employment I realized I didn't want to have to do this ever again. In my mind, I equated my poor showing in the classroom at Duquesne with my job at the beer distributor. I didn't want a future of beer delivery jobs, and I knew the only way to ensure that was to do well with my studies.

My career on the beer truck ended up in August, and I went back to school with a new attitude. That attitude consisted of sitting in the front row for each of my classes and using tutors for the really tough classes. I also borrowed a learning tip I learned from studying drama. I was taught to reread a play numerous times in order to memorize lines and to write and rewrite my character's lines from a play to speed up the memorization process. I started to reread my textbook assignments three and four times, and I rewrote each day's notes from each class. Highlighter pen markings could be found everywhere throughout my books and in my notes. Almost every Saturday afternoon was spent studying in the library. In addition to the books and articles I was reading on economics I began to read each issue of *Business*

Week. My parents never knew how close I came to leaving college, and I was going to do everything possible to prevent them from finding out.

The Grade Point Average for my second semester was over 2.0. And for the remaining five semesters I was enrolled at Duquesne my GPA was higher than the preceding semester. One semester, I even nailed a 3.4. And this was at an institution that didn't hand out any gift grades to students.

Each semester, each month, each week that went by I could feel my comprehension and my understanding of the subject of economics and my familiarity with well-known economists increase dramatically. Because of their connection to economics, the finance, marketing, business law and accounting classes became less difficult for me.

My command of the English language isn't great enough to describe to you the incredible feeling of joy and satisfaction I had when I reached the point where I realized that I would be graduating from college. The great thing about the feeling was that it lasted from the beginning of my last semester until after I graduated. I just hope that in your life you have moments that give you the same feeling I had when I realized I would graduate. If I could describe to you in one short sentence what happened to me from the time I finished my first semester at Duquesne, to the time I applied to transfer and decided against it, to the time I realized that driving a beer truck wasn't for me to the time I was able to master the class work is this: I learned how to learn. I learned how to separate valid and relevant information from worthless or junk data. I learned how to do research in the most effective and efficient manner possible, and I learned how to focus on a subject in preparation for an exam. Of all the benefits of education, the ability to learn is arguably the greatest one of all.

The other college experience I value has nothing to do with the classes I took or the people I met. It was that moment when I was considering transferring to another school and realized that no matter what it took, no matter what price I paid, I had to stay at Duquesne and finish. The fact that I stood up to the challenge and came out victorious was just as important, if not more so, than getting the level and quality of education I did.

I left college with a lot of things in my favor: knowledge, ambition, persistence and a great desire to create, achieve and accomplish. The one thing I didn't have going for me was a job.

My job search started before my last semester. I had written a term paper about the 1948 antitrust case against the motion picture studios and had submitted it to the local sales person for the now defunct motion picture company United Artists. This gentleman arranged for me to have a job interview in New York City based on my interest in the motion picture industry. I traveled to New York in early January the same way I did when I went to apply for drama school...by Greyhound bus. I had the interview but did not get a job. I did, however, enjoy my short visit to New York and even stayed in the same transient hotel I had stayed in four years earlier. On the bus ride home, I was filled with anticipation and excitement for my last semester of college.

During my last semester I sent resumes to the major corporations in town and to numerous companies across the country;especially companies I had read about in business publications. Unfortunately, I received no positive response from my resumes. That didn't bother me at the time because I was confident that the on-campus interview process would result in me landing a great job.

For those of you who never participated in on-campus interviews the process works like this: Sign-up sheets are posted in the college's placement office with about twenty openings. Students stop by the office and sign up for any company with which they wish to interview. There are always more students trying to get an interview than openings so it is competitive just to get on the calendar. If you were lucky enough to get on the schedule, you would go to the library to do some research on the company, prepare a list of questions to ask the interviewer and wear a suit and tie to class on the day of the interview.

At the time, I owned only one suit. The suit I had was a hand-me down from my older brother. It was a brown double-knit polyester suit. My suit looked like it was a cousin of the leisure suit. At the time, it didn't bother me. Any interviewer was certainly going to look past the quality of my suit and realize that I had a gift for the subject of economics and tremendous drive, ambition and persistence...qualities that any company looks for, right?

No. Not right. The interviews I went on consisted of me sitting across from an individual who gave the impression he or she would rather be any place than in that room. The questions I was asked had nothing to do with my knowledge or insight or ambition. The questions were basic and general. "Where do I want to be five years from now?" "How would you describe yourself?" "How would others describe you?" "If you were a tree, what kind of tree would you be?"

The interviewers didn't care about my knowledge of economics. They didn't care that I could discuss the writings of Irving Fisher, John Maynard Keynes, Paul Samuelson, Karl Marx, John Kenneth Galbraith, Milton Friedman, Adam Smith, John Stuart Mill, etc. They didn't care that I could quote the Theory of Interest, the complex Yield-To-Maturity formula, the demand function, the law of diminishing returns, demand elasticities and inelasticities, and marginal revenue/cost formulations from memory. They only saw an overly ambitious young man who took a unique route through college wearing his older brother's brown double-knit polyester suit.

My on-campus interviews resulted in a batch of "Dear Ken" rejection letters.

I left college with no job, no car (my car had been totaled) and no money. On the day I graduated from Duquesne I posed for pictures with my parents and the two women who worked in the Academic Advisors office (I had seen them so often during my time at Duquesne, and they had removed me from academic probation only two weeks before graduation). My parents took me to lunch at a restaurant in Oakland and then we went home. That was it. I was a college graduate.

There is one story I want to end this chapter with. There was a young man I will refer to as Matt who was at Community College with me and transferred to Duquesne at the same time. He was a good looking kid who dressed cool and seemingly always had a lit Marlboro in his hand. Matt had gone to a high school close to mine and told me the names of the girls from my school he had dated. The list was impressive. We had much in common because of the neighborhoods we came from, our time spent at Community College and our shared difficult time getting through the business school at Duquesne.

Matt had gotten involved with the on-campus interview process. Like me, he only owned one suit. Unlike mine, his suit was a good-looking suit. He was going on interviews and meeting the same results as me.

One day, a sign-up sheet was posted in the Job Placement office. Eastman Kodak was coming to campus for interviews. I was excited because of my interest in the motion picture industry. I also had working knowledge of film speeds, film emulsions and was a regular reader of a newsletter published by Kodak that detailed film products and their use in filmmaking. I was able to get a slot on the sign-up sheet right above Matt.

The day of the Kodak interview was a warm spring day. It was a day similar to the day I made my first daytime visit to the campus and strolled along Academic Walk. I put on my brown double-knit polyester suit with a new tie my mother had bought me. The suit and tie combination, coupled with my enthusiasm for the Kodak interview, gave me confidence in my appearance.

As I strolled across the campus that day I saw Matt walking toward me. He was not wearing his suit. Instead he was dressed in his customary jeans, T-shirt and clogs and smoking a Marlboro. When we met in the middle of Academic Walk, our conversation went something like this:

ME:
Don't tell me you forgot.

MATT:
Forgot what?

ME:
Today's the big day. The Kodak interview day.

MATT:
I didn't forget, Ken. I'm just sick and tired of wearing that same suit to class all day long, going in for a twenty minute interview and being asked a bunch of pointless questions.

ME:

So you're going to blow off a job interview with Eastman Kodak?

MATT:

Oh, I'm still going to the interview.

ME:

Dressed like that?

MATT:

That's right. But I came prepared.

And with that he pulled a photograph of himself out of his notebook and showed it to me. In the photo he was wearing his suit and tie.

MATT:

I'm going to show this to the interviewer when I walk into the office. They'll see how I look when I'm dressed up.

At the conclusion of this chapter, I want to ask you a question that I will answer at the beginning of the next chapter. *Do you think my friend got the job at Kodak?*

> In the deepest, darkest depths of winter,
> I learned there lay within me an
> invincible summer.
>
> — *Albert Camus (French novelist;1913-1960)*

Matt did not get a job with Eastman Kodak. The creativity and initiative Matt showed by bringing his 'suit and tie' photo to the interview was not what Kodak was looking for. (I've told this story to business owners and executives of large companies. They all told me the same thing. They would not necessarily have hired Matt for doing what he did, but they would have given him a closer look).

I did not get a job with Kodak either. I left college with no job offer. That didn't worry me. Armed with my degree and my desire to get on any rung of the corporate ladder, I hit the job market hard. I started sending out resumes in response to ads from the newspaper and phoning employment agencies to arrange interviews.

The first batch of resumes I sent out were met with rejection letters or no replies. The ads placed by employment agencies ended the same way. It would turn out that the job I called about had been filled or I was deemed unqualified for. The agent would then tell me about another job opening they had and attempt to steer me to that position. It was their version of the classic 'bait and switch.' I remember having a heated discussion with an employee of one of these firms who wanted to send me on an interview for a job as the assistant manager of a shoe store. When I told him I wasn't interested in working at a shoe store, he tried to convince me it was a great job because it had free parking and I would learn how to use a cash register.

As spring became summer I was still without employment. The rejection I received during each week would be replaced by newfound enthusiasm each Sunday evening. This was the time I set aside to read the help wanted ads. I would go through the ads two times and circle the ads I was interested in. I would then type up cover letters for each ad on the small Smith-Corona typewriter my mother had bought for our family when my older brother entered high school. I would try to customize each letter to show I had some knowledge and interest in the business that placed the ad. Before putting the letter with a resume into an envelope I would make sure I folded the pages so they would come out of the envelope right side up. I tried to make everything easy for whoever was reading my cover letter in the Human Resources Department.

After the letters were prepared I would walk to the mailbox at the top of our street. Before putting the letters in the box, I would flip through them, making sure again that the stamps were secure and there were no misspellings. I would almost pray over the letters hoping that one would find its way to a Human Resources employee who appreciated my ambition, my desire to work and my knowledge of economics. I would then drop the letters into the box and walk back home.

Unfortunately, my prayers and hopes were never answered. I got few interviews from the resumes I sent. What I received mostly were more "Dear Ken" rejection letters. The letters promised that my resume would be kept on file and, if a suitable position were to open, I would be contacted for an interview. I seriously doubt that my resumes were kept in any file.

I received numerous rejection letters. I received letters without my name on them and I received letters addressed to other people. I even received rejection letters from companies that I did not send a resume to. I have two theories on how this happened. My first theory is that the placement office at Duquesne was sending my resume to various companies on my behalf. Even though I didn't know where my resumes were going, and even though the receiving company had no interest in hiring me, they would still go to the trouble of sending me a rejection letter.

The second theory is a bit more sinister. Because I was getting rejection letters from firms that I hadn't applied to I envisioned that Human Resource workers traded resumes with HR workers from other companies so they could increase the number of rejection letters being sent. They would get together on a regular basis around a circular table and distribute copies of resumes received since the last meeting. They would then go back to their respective offices and send out a new batch of rejection letters to job seekers. (I know this second theory sounds silly but having dealt with HR Directors through my various business activities, I can't help but think there is a hint of reality in it).

The employment agencies and want ads weren't paying off for me so I picked up my job search. I began visiting two different State Job Service offices on a regular basis to review the job openings posted in the microfiche machines and on the note cards posted around the room. At the time I was in these offices, there was a major recession going on in the country. The offices were usually crowded with job seekers. What made it interesting was the range of job seekers. The recession put a wide variety of workers in the unemployment line. As I walked around the room reading the job openings, I could find myself standing next to an electrical engineer or a janitor. I remember once overhearing two people at a table looking at the obituary section of the newspaper trying to see if the place of employment was listed for any of the deceased. This was their response to the tough job market.

I did get a few job interviews from this process, but the item I remember most was when one of the counselors reviewed my resume and suggested that I get some retraining. I told her I would like the chance to use the business training I had just received from Duquesne University before getting retrained.

My determination to find employment was so strong that I tried non-traditional ways to find a job. A few of my job search approaches are listed below for your review (and amusement):

The Office Building Approach—This approach consisted of putting on my suit and tie and taking a bunch of resumes to office building complexes throughout the Pittsburgh area. I would hand-deliver a resume to each office and attempt to see a person of authority while I was there. I covered the downtown area as well as the west, north, south and east parts of the city. This method didn't work for me at all as I got no response to my resumes and never made it in to see anybody in charge of anything. My best (or worst) memories of this exercise were twofold: I once was driving home from the eastern part of town and stopped at a gas station. At the time I only had 37 cents on me and all of it went into the gas tank. I still remember the look the attendant gave me as I put the money in her hand. Maybe she would have given me a more understanding look if I had told her I once pumped gas at a Texaco station. Another time, while in the downtown area, I was standing at a crosswalk waiting for the light to change. An older woman was standing next to me, and I noticed her looking at me. I turned and gave her a short smile. She smiled back and asked me if my suit (yes, the same quasi-leisure suit) was the type of suit you could run through the washing machine.

The Duquesne Club Approach—One day before lunch I positioned myself outside of the dapper Duquesne Club at 11:30 a.m. and started to pass out resumes as the executives pulled up in their limos and Cadillacs and entered the club. Some of the people I gave my resume to seemed genuinely interested in what I was doing but my time in front of the club was limited. Somebody from the club sent the doorman outside to chase me away. I attempted to appeal to the doorman to cut me a break and let me stay five more minutes but as he stood at the top of the steps in his doorman uniform he wasn't open to hear any appeals.

The Stockbroker Approach—Although I didn't obtain my investment license until after I was out of college for a few years, I actually attempted to become a broker in the months right after graduation. On one of my trips to the city I visited a handful of brokerage firms and left resumes. I received no follow-up calls, but one sales manager of a large office agreed to see me. I was ushered in past the desks of brokers and their assistants. The manager's office was large and a woman was measuring him for a new suit. We talked about my background and he questioned me about stocks, bonds, etc. After the tailor left, the sales manager gave me his honest and frank opinion about the best way for me to become a broker. His advice to me was "to get a job selling used cars for five years and then come back to see me." (My attempts to become a broker right after graduation will play a part a little later in this story. Stay tuned.)

As the end of summer approached, I was still without a job. I worked part-time at a film lab in Pittsburgh and did construction labor work whenever I could. My parents were great to me during this time. My mother would give me suggestions on applying for jobs and gave me the names of companies and temporary agencies I should contact. My father would always tell me not to worry about not having a job, and he respected the fact I was trying as hard as I knew how to find one. He told me more than once that I just had some bad luck by graduating into a recession. I would try to tell him that the recession was not keeping me out of work;it was the way the system operated that was keeping me out of a job. My time spent looking for work beginning in my last semester of college and continuing into the months after graduation made me realize that the corporate ladder I was trying so hard to get a foothold on didn't exist. What existed in its place was a corporate escalator. And young men who stumbled through high school, detoured through Community College on their way to a mediocre showing at Duquesne wearing double-knit brown suits and their ambition on their sleeve were not invited to ride that escalator. If I had known I was going to be in for this much rejection, I just might have continued to pursue an acting career.

My father would do a generous and kind thing for me. He would send me to the store to buy him a case of beer or a few items from the grocery store and hand me a $10 or $20 bill and tell me to keep the change. Often that change would end up at the local shot and beer bar with me sipping 75 cent drafts with my friends who had not yet moved out of town and planning my next strategy for locating a job.

My parents' house was a great salvation to me. Some days I would hike in the woods behind the house trying to keep my confidence level up and trying to blow off the frustration of being unemployed. Other days I would sit on the porch and read various books and magazines on business and the subject of economics. Although I wasn't working, I never walked away from my reading habit. I was still a regular visitor to the Duquesne University library.

There was one time when I was so close to a job that the taste of employment was in my mouth. In November, six months after graduating, I received a phone call from a large financial services company located downtown. The woman in the Human Resources Department invited me in for a job interview.

After a brief interview with the woman in HR, I was led to the office of a gentleman in the customer service department. He and I had a great conversation. The interview was tremendously encouraging. It went so well that the person I interviewed with asked me if I would be willing to talk to another person that same day. What was I going to say? Of course I stayed in town and met with the second person. That interview went as well as the previous one, and I was told I would be given a call in a few days to set up another interview. That call came, and I was back downtown for my third interview. Once again, during that interview, I was asked to stay in the building to have another interview. And once again, that interview went well. I was told that I would be interviewing with one of the high ranking executives. At this time in the process I was excited because it was getting close to Christmas, and I was thinking that the anguish of the past six months could be erased with the simple words, "You're hired."

Here's where this story takes a plot twist. Instead of receiving a call to interview with this executive, I received a rejection letter. I phoned my contact in the HR Department and asked if a mistake had been made. I mentioned the name of the last person I had interviewed with and the name of the person I was supposed to meet. She promised to get back in touch with me.

A few days later she called and asked if I could be back in the building the following week. I breathed a sigh of relief as my job hunt got back on track. I had that interview and returned home to wait for some good news. I was on edge every day waiting for the phone to ring or a letter to arrive telling me what day I would start working. And then it arrived.

Two days before Christmas I received a letter from the woman in the HR Department. I literally (and I mean 'literally') knelt down and said a prayer before opening it. Please, please, let it be a job offer.

It wasn't an offer of employment. It was another damned rejection letter. I immediately phoned the woman. I was told she was unavailable. She never returned the phone call or the other calls I made to her.

It stinks to go through a long interview process for a job paying $14,400 per year and have the process end abruptly with a rejection letter. And it really stinks to get that letter two days before Christmas.

I was disappointed with the way I was treated by this company and by the woman in the HR Department who had set me up to be an "interview whore" and then wouldn't return my phone calls. My disappointment turned to anger and, as a way to rid myself of the anger, I needed to do something to let this person know how I felt. Without telling you exactly what I did, I was able to vent my frustration and anger. What I did was not in poor taste or rude. What I did actually showed class, creativity and style. I have told my "interview whore" story numerous times and actually make it sound funnier than it was. And the woman from this company probably still thinks about me every so often.

The new year came with me still looking for work. The Sunday paper, the state job service, the employment agencies--I continued to pursue them all. But none of them resulted in a job offer. Some of my friends from high school had since moved to Houston where a major job boom was taking place. If I would have had the financial ability to move I probably would have said good-bye to Pittsburgh at this time and gone to Texas to stay with one of my friends. But I had no traveling money and no car of my own. I was using my family's second car to look for jobs.

I never wavered from my determination to get a job. Even after being jobless for such an extended period of time I saw myself as a talented, knowledgeable, ambitious individual...what you're supposed to be when you are hunting for a career. The problem was not with me, the problem was with the system. The way companies looked for employees was hurting me. I was a little too ambitious, too driven. Companies that operate on conformity don't like that.

I have no recollection of my birthday that year. It came and went as did my first anniversary of being a college graduate. Unemployment was not a good birthday or anniversary present.

Finally, and I mean finally, I got a job. More than a year since I had graduated from Duquesne University I was offered a full-time, cash paying job. I was working.

Now, before you applaud, wait until you hear where I got a job.

The best defense is a good offense.
— Richard Harding (8th & 9th grade wrestling coach)

The job I got as a result of my intense experience at Duquesne and the thousand plus resumes I sent out and the countless telephone calls, hand-delivered resumes and scores of interviews was...get ready for this...with a company that installed swimming pools. That's right. I was back working at the same type of job that led to my enrollment at Community College and my travels through the world of higher education. But this time, it was much different.

I started working for a company that had little in common with my previous pool company. This company built an inferior pool, had equipment and workers of a lower quality and paid less than the previous company. It ticked me off to no end that I had to go back to pick and shovel work after all the hard work I put into my studies.

But things were about to change for me. This sentence you are reading right now is a vital plot point in this story.

I was with the new company for a few weeks and had to drag myself to work each day. Each eight-hour day seemed like an eternity. When I got off work, it seemed like only a few minutes would pass before I had to drag myself back to work for the next day's drudgery. I hated this job.

One day I found myself working in the deep end of a pool shaping the walls in order to install the liner. And it happened. Another epiphany. The light bulb went on above my head. It suddenly dawned on me that every one of those resumes I sent to a Human Resources Director or to the Personnel Department had been a waste of my time. Those people certainly could not understand or appreciate who I was and the ambition I had. My knowledge and drive was beyond their level of comprehension and I was unlike the typical conformist employee they were used to. I realized at that moment that I had to apply directly to somebody who could relate to me--the owners of companies. Because I never lost my interest in real estate development and the idea of building things for people, I decided to send resumes directly to the owners of real estate development firms. The local newspaper and business newspaper regularly put the names of developers and information about their projects in articles, and I was reading these articles on a regular basis.

When I climbed out of the hopper that day, I went home and listed the names of five Pittsburgh real estate developers who were going to get a letter and resume from me. Probably as a direct result of the enormous amount of resumes and cover letters I had sent out, my family's small electric typewriter was not in working order. I had to go to the Duquesne library and use one of their machines.

I composed a sincere cover letter and sent it out to the five developers. Within one week I received a telephone call from the secretary of one of the developers. She said her boss wanted to talk to me. Could I be in their office in two days? Without worrying about the consequences of taking a day off of my job, I said yes.

On the day of the interview I drove to the address I was given. It was an apartment building located in the Oakland section of Pittsburgh. The office I entered was a converted first floor apartment. It was not the most impressive office setting. In what had once been somebody's living room, a group of bookkeepers was tabulating rent checks, paying bills and conducting the business of a real estate office.

I entered the office of the company owner. He was dressed casually, and his office was decorated with photos of his airplane and shots taken from the plane. We sat across from each other at his desk and he explained to me that he had been successful in the real estate business and had been thinking of hiring someone to help him research new businesses he wanted to start. He also wanted to buy businesses and needed somebody to help him do the due diligence on potential acquisitions. My resume had crossed his desk at the right time. We talked in great detail about my studies and my interest in real estate development and the investment business. To test my knowledge, he asked me to tell him how I would go about performing research on the bicycle industry. Without skipping a beat I started talking about the information that could be found through bicycle or sporting goods trade groups, through the review of 10-K Statements and Annual Reports of publicly-traded companies that make and market bicycles and through contact with various export/import agencies to measure the amount of bikes sold overseas or imported into America. As I went on and on I remember standing up and pacing across the room as my creative juices flowed. I looked down at the developer as I talked about studying the past and current methods used to build and market bikes and determining the future of the industry by studying demographics and the demand of the complementary items associated with the industry.

When I sat back down I could tell he was impressed with my thoroughness. He told me he would consider hiring me only if I wrote a three-page summary of my background, abilities, and what value I could add to his business. That night I was back at the Duquesne library writing the report. It was hand delivered to their offices early the next morning before I went off to install another low-quality swimming pool.

A few nights later I received a follow-up call from the secretary. She wanted to know if I could be in their offices early the next morning. I didn't even bother calling the owner of the pool company and telling him to start without me in the morning.

I told my parents I had an interview in the morning but didn't tell them that this was a second interview. Because the car I was using was unreliable and had a history of breaking down, I made arrangements with my father to drive him to work in the morning, use his car for the interview, and pick him up after work.

I drove my father to work early the next morning and hurried home to take a shower and put on my suit. I drove back to the apartment building/office twenty minutes in advance of the interview and waited outside. Fortunately, my father's car had air conditioning that worked and I kept it running until it was time for my meeting.

When I sat in the developer's office, he looked at me and simply said, "I got a job for you." When he said that to me, I felt the weight of the world leave my shoulders and the heavy pressure I had been carrying inside leave my chest. I had a job.

The developer told me what my first projects were going to be and what my salary would be. He introduced me to his secretary and instructed her to help me obtain any research materials I needed. He would be going out of town for two weeks and would check in with me periodically to discuss my projects.

When I left the office, I was walking on air. I got home and told my mother the news and asked her not to tell my father anything if he should happen to call.

My father worked for the gas company in a substation in the North Side of Pittsburgh. As far back as I could remember this is where my father worked. My brothers and I had been going there since we were kids, and we had grown up knowing the procedures and happenings at the plant and the details of my father's co-workers. We were also familiar with the incredible loud and constant noise made by the plant's boilers, chillers and compressors. Twenty years of this noise had cost my father a good bit of his hearing.

When I strolled into the plant I didn't let on about my new job to my father or anybody else in the control room. The co-workers were all familiar with my situation and on occasion sent home job search suggestions with my father for me to pursue.

My father and I left the plant and walked back to the car. I made small talk with him and offered to drive him home. As we were pulling out of the parking lot in the blue Olds Delta Royale, I simply and casually remarked to my father, "About that job interview I had today...I got that job." My father was silent for a moment and then said, "That's good. Now show them what you can do." I will tell you this right now: it has been a good number of years since my futile job search and anguish caused by it. As I write this section the memories and the associated feelings all come rushing back to me. But what also comes back to me is the joy I felt when I told my father I had a job. How I wish I could have that moment...my father sitting next to me in his blue work shirt from Equitable Gas Company and me steering his car onto Federal Street on a warm spring day...to live over again.

Before I get into the details of my job and how it relates to this book, I want to share something with you. Being unable to find a job after college was embarrassing, painful and often times degrading. But as the years pass by and my knowledge of my chosen fields increases and my abilities expand exponentially, the embarrassment, pain and degradation diminishes. I can talk and speak of my experiences with only a hint of the anger that used to form in my stomach as I talked about Human Resource Departments, resumes and interviews. I have told my story in seminars and even managed to get laughter when I reveal my identity as the "interview whore." I also want to share something that dawned on me as I was preparing this chapter. Many people have had to endure hardships much more difficult than I did. The sacrifices my parents and other parents made for their children were ten times more difficult than the temporary situation I found myself in. In fact, I can now make the statement that my bout with being out of work was good for me. It made me more aggressive, more creative and it confirmed my confidence in my knowledge. It made me become a person who realizes the importance of taking initiative and being persistent. I was lucky to acquire these traits at such a young age. I will also tell you that if you think any part of this story so far is interesting, there are experiences and insights I've benefitted from as a result of my unemployment that I left off these pages. And some of these experiences and insights are more interesting than what you've read or are about to read. I don't know the person I would have become if the company that interviewed me six times gave me a job. I do know the person I have become, and I'll ride with him into the future.

I started my new job with a great assignment. My boss wanted to open his own bank in the state of Florida, and I was assigned to find out every procedure, rule and nuance in establishing a savings institution. I ended up becoming extensively involved in every aspect of starting a bank from finding an attorney to file the paperwork, to finding an economist to do the primary service area study to finding a location for the bank. I am telling you this because it enables me to tell you this: two months after I was in the deep end of the swimming pool and got the idea of applying directly to real estate developers, I made the first of many trips to Tampa, Florida. Four months after I got the idea, I made an extended trip to various Caribbean islands to research sites for possible housing and hotel developments. In case you were wondering, my brown double-knit polyester suit was tossed out upon the receipt of my first paycheck. If there was such a place as the Bad Suit Hall of Fame, that suit would be there. To this day, I never wear brown clothes.

In addition to working at the bank and overseeing various banking functions in Pittsburgh, I was in charge of a variety of functions for my company. The foundation of the business was a real estate development company, and my boss kept giving me more and more responsibilities as he saw I was able to handle to work. I became the site acquisition, leasing, and commercial mortgage department. As I got more involved in real estate transactions and entered into more and more serious negotiations with sellers, tenants, borrowers and lenders, my boss instilled in me a sense that the people I was dealing with were going to be supplying me with information. Some of the information was going to be valid and relevant to the subject being discussed, but much of the information was going to be supplied in an attempt to divert me from the true value or condition of a property, financial condition of a seller, buyer or borrower. I developed an incredibly useful talent in separating fact from fiction and substance from hype. I became able to separate a person telling me the truth from a person trying to mislead me or hiding relevant information from me. This skill has become the basis of any activity I am involved in...inside or outside the world of business.

One of my favorite projects consisted of the establishment of a multi-million dollar leveraged bond portfolio. I was given the task of interviewing various investment banking firms in Pittsburgh to oversee the structure, selection and management of a corporate bond portfolio that was to be used by my employer for income tax purposes. I donned one of my new suits and went from firm to firm inquiring about their research ability, fee structure, and the expertise of the people who would actually be managing the portfolio. This was one of my favorite projects because it was those same investment firms that I visited in search of a job during my extensive search for employment. The shoe...or the suit...was now on the other foot. The same people who wouldn't see me when I came to inquire about a job were now ushering me into their conference rooms and were overly nice to me as they gave me their pitch to manage the bond portfolio. The gentleman who had told me to get a job selling used cars couldn't refill my coffee cup fast enough. *(After a review of the investment managers in Pittsburgh, the contract was given to an asset manager in New York City).*

My job provided me with unique insight into the real estate, banking and investment industries. It "forced" me into developing a totally objective mind. That objectivity has been of incredible assistance in my continuing education process, in my decision making ability and in my creativity. The balance of this book will consist of me sharing my financial insight and my objective realizations of how the investment business really works...and how it should work. As I write this I am especially looking forward to sharing with you the unique connection between the banking business, the real estate business and the investment business and how that connection often results in improper investment decisions by an uninformed and unwary public.

Before I share my journey through the investment business with you and get to the heart of this book, I want to leave you with an insight I acquired during my intensive and extensive job search. Go back to that moment when I was standing in the deep end of the hole that was about to become a swimming pool. When I received the epiphany that I should not look for a job by contacting people in the Human Resources Departments of companies but should be contacting the owners of real estate companies directly, I received another insight at the same time.

My second epiphany was this: my efforts in securing employment by submitting resumes to personnel people was a royal waste of my time and efforts. Here I was, a young man full of ambition, enthusiasm and an incredible desire to create, achieve and accomplish putting myself in front of a group of people who were not ambitious, not interested in creating, achieving and accomplishing and not interested in letting the rest of the world know they're here. The Human Resources people who received my resume and immediately threw a rejection letter into an envelope and sent it to me or the people who gave me an interview because it would kill some time for them during their non-busy work day had one thing in common: their collective futures were behind them. And my future was bright and glaring and right in front of me for the taking. So I am going to end this chapter with another quote. This quote was written by me and it was born as a result of my dealings with Human Resources people and other people who get in the way of those who have an inherent need to make something of themselves. Here it is:

Never let your future get behind you.

- Ken Kaszak

The price one pays for pursuing any profession, or calling, is an intimate knowledge of its ugly side.

— James Baldwin (American novelist;1924-1987)

Three and a half years after going to work for the real estate developer who pulled me out of the swimming pool hopper and put me to work, I was faced with a major decision. I had always lived in Pittsburgh and traveled to Florida and other cities in durations of one or two week stays, but the bank I had helped start in Tampa was at the stage where it needed the full time attention of me or somebody who could do the variety of tasks I was doing. My boss came into my office one day and told me he needed me to relocate to Tampa and wanted me to move there.

As I thought over the decision to move I remembered the great times I had in Tampa, the newness and beauty of the city, the street level ground floor office I worked out of at the bank, the nightclubs and bars, and the people I had met. I thought about my experiences in the city and I thought about how much I enjoyed staying at the downtown Hyatt Hotel with the swimming pool on the roof.

But I also thought about how much I liked Pittsburgh, how much I liked driving my jet black Z-28 around town, and I thought about how I always had a case of homesickness when I went on a trip. I had also developed an interest in other ventures that I wanted to pursue in my city. The fact that I had walked around my hometown jobless for a long time after graduating from college didn't even enter the equation. After a few days of thinking over my options I told my boss I was going to stay in Pittsburgh.

Fortunately for me, I was able to reach a deal to continue doing investment research for my boss' company on a part-time basis. This part-time income would prove instrumental in keeping me afloat as I got involved in my new business.

That new business was in the cable-TV business;specifically the business of private cable television. Private cable is the part of the industry where apartment building owners own the cable service feeding their buildings or sell their cable rights to a private operator. It was common in large cities like Tampa, Los Angeles and Dallas for apartment owners to increase the revenue from their properties by operating the cable-TV service. I had always had an interest in every aspect of the broadcasting industry and had met most of the apartment building owners in Pittsburgh. My thinking at the time was that I would be the first person to introduce private cable to the local building owners. *(There is a reason why I'm sharing this information. My knowledge of the cable television industry has direct impact to my experience in the investment business. You will soon find out how and why.)*

Almost immediately after I set up my own operation, I met a fellow who had the same idea that I did. He had all the technical knowledge of satellite television installation and operation and I had the marketing knowledge and real estate contacts. We set out to install cable-TV systems in apartment buildings throughout the Pittsburgh area.

Luck was on our side early on. We got a contract to build and operate a cable system at a 465-unit building located near the Pittsburgh Airport. The building was brand new and was being built by a company from Texas. Private cable was common in Texas. At the time, we thought this was going to be the first of many properties contracting with us to install private cable.

Unfortunately, things didn't work out that way. Although I personally knew or knew by reputation every major apartment building owner in Pittsburgh, we couldn't interest any of them to install their own cable system or sell us the cable rights for their building. The business evolved into a small entity that operated the one system and installed satellite equipment for other vendors.

One day I was driving back from the building where our system was located. There were construction delays on my way back into the city, and I got off a different exit to take the detour. I was in a section of town I had never been in. As I pondered whether or not there was a future in private cable-TV in Pittsburgh or if my cable venture was going to be stuck permanently in neutral, I drove past a small office building. There was a large sign indicating that the building housed an investment company. But what was most impressive was the line-up in the parking lot. There was a top-of-the-line Mercedes, a Corvette, and a Porsche 944. Who ever was in that building selling investments was selling enough of them to keep some nice cars on the road.

I pulled into the parking lot. Dressed in work boots and jeans I walked into the office and told the receptionist I wanted to become a stockbroker. She asked me to wait in the lobby and disappeared up a staircase. In a few minutes she reappeared and was followed by a sharply dressed gentleman. He introduced himself and led me into a conference room.

It turns out he was the owner of the Corvette and worked for the husband and wife team who owned the company. They wanted to dramatically expand the number of brokers who were selling invest-ments on behalf of the company. I explained my educational background and work history. I also explained that I had been extensively re-searching various investments and ventures for my ex-employer and shared my experience in the banking industry. I knew I made a posi-tive impression on the interviewer even though I wasn't dressed for the part.

Without having to submit a resume or fill out an application, I was told that I could enter the company's training program. The training program, coupled with my self-studying and previous knowledge, would prepare me to take the NASD Series 7 license examination. The test was given nationally once each month. I had the option of taking the test to be given in two weeks or waiting until the following month.

Given the fact I was a young man with no patience I stood up at the end of the interview with my new colleague and announced that I would be ready to take the test in two weeks.

Over the next two weeks my days and nights were filled with preparation for the Series 7 test. I was living in a one-bedroom apartment on the South Side at the time. In the mornings I would leave my apartment and drive to the offices of the investment company for required training classes that lasted all morning. I would race home in the afternoon and tear into my studying program. Early in the evening I would take a break from studying for a quick swim or some pick-up basketball at the outdoor court and then go right home for more studying. I studied straight through until a little after midnight and would take a break. My break consisted of a walk to the local convenience store for a cup of coffee. Upon my return home I would study until around 4:00 in the morning and then grab a few hours of sleep before I started over.

The training in the basement of the investment company consisted of classes on how to prospect for clients, the mechanics of margin accounts and option transactions. I don't have many memories of those classes but one burning memory is the temperature. The combination of no air conditioning, the month of August and ten people crowded around a table made for steamy conditions.

The test was given on a Saturday. I studied late into the evening on Friday. My brain was crammed with securities laws, upticks, downticks, spreads, straddles, puts, calls, interest rate movements, etc. About two o'clock in the morning, I took a walk down to 18th Street for a cup of coffee. I remember that walk for this reason: as I passed 20th Street, a young man staggered around the corner. Judging from the way he walked, it was not hard to see he had been drinking, and drinking heavily, at one of the Carson Street bars. As he came around the corner, he stumbled and tripped. He landed on the sidewalk with a thud. As I looked at him sprawled on the ground I thought that 9,999 times out of 10,000 I would run over and make sure he was all right and see if he needed any help. But the night before the Series 7 exam was the one time I was not going to do that. Although I have a great reputation for feeding stray dogs and handing out money to homeless people, I could not interrupt my schedule. I continued my walk to the convenience store. *(On my way back to my apartment I did notice that the fellow had gotten up and walked away or was helped up by someone else.)*

At the time, the Series 7 exam was given at Duquesne University. I thought that was a positive omen. The other positive omens were that the test was given in a classroom where a few of my business school classes were held, and the moderator for the test was a professor at Duquesne who was my teacher for two classes *(No, it was not the professor who suggested I return to Community College).*

The test is an 8-hour test and covers numerous topics related to the proper and legal way to deal with customers, what can and cannot be said to prospective clients, advertising, the history of the stock and bond markets, options, margins, etc. There are five sections to the test, and the questions for each section are interspersed throughout the test.

In the morning part of the exam I got stuck on some questions and spent way too much time trying to answer them. There were questions about bond interest payments that required mathematic calculations that I was not prepared for. The questions on margin accounts almost buried me. At the lunch break I remember thinking that taking only two weeks to study for this test was not enough time.

The afternoon session did not go any better. There were questions that I answered and then went back and changed the answer only to go back again and revert to the original answer. I sweated over every question and cursed myself for taking only two weeks to study.

The test ended at 4:00 in the afternoon. I got up from my chair at 3:55. I forced a smile as I handed my test to my ex-teacher, and he wished me well. I drove to my parents' house after the test. Even their encouraging words could not help me erase the feeling of how badly I had done on the exam.

A week and a half after the test I was instructed to call a phone number to see if I'd passed or failed. The number was a toll number and at the time my telephone service was restricted to local calls only. I ended up getting about $2.00 in change and walking to the payphone on the side of Stutz's Drug Store. I threw the change in the phone and called the number. I supplied my name and Social Security number to the gentleman who answered the phone. He put me on hold for a few moments and then came back on the line.

The first thing I heard was, "Congratulations, you passed." I was stunned. From the moment I opened my exam booklet to the very moment I made the phone call I was convinced that I had failed the exam. I was now a stockbroker, an investment broker, an investment advisor, a financial planner. Any of those terms could now be used to describe me, the owner of a Series 7 NASD license. Before I hung up the phone, I was told that only 12% of the people across the country who took the test the day I did passed it. Often when I drive past that pay phone on the side of Stutz's drugstore I fondly recall myself making that phone call.

When I reported back to work at the investment company, I signed my employment contract. My contract stipulated that I was an independent contractor and would be responsible for all of my expenses. I would be paid 40% of the commissions I generated for the company and the company would retain 60%. The contract further stated that if I left the company for any reason, or was asked to leave, I would not be allowed to sell investments for any other brokerage firm within a 60 mile radius of the company's offices.

I was assigned a tin desk in the upstairs section of the building. Because this company was trying to grow, the owners had expanded the building and created room for about 15 brokers upstairs in the addition. On top of my desk was a telephone, a telephone book and a blotter. I was told to generate a list of 100 prospects that I could call to discuss financial planning.

Now here was my situation. I had my license, and I had a tremendous amount of enthusiasm and energy for the investment business. What I didn't have was anybody I could sell investments to. My ex-boss, whom I was in contact with on a regular basis, was interested in giving me more work assignments but no money to invest. My family and friends, hard working and honest people, weren't in a financial position to invest money.

I began to compile my list with the names of the individuals I had met in the real estate and construction industries. I added the names of acquaintances who I thought might have some money to invest. I worked on my list for one week but was far short of the 100 names I was required to come up with. When I told the person who had been given the title of Marketing Manager at the firm that I was having trouble coming up with 100 names, he did something that would be repeated in the movie *Wall Street*. He pointed at the telephone book on my desk and told me there was plenty of prospects for me to contact.

I did add random names and phone numbers from the telephone book, and I did call most of the people on my list, even the ones whose names I picked from the phone book. But I got no appointments...even with the real estate and construction people I had met while working in that business. Nobody I talked to was interested in talking to me about financial planning. I would arrive at the office, sit at my tin desk and muster the energy I needed to make my phone calls. When I exhausted the names on my first list, I would create a new list and start over. I would brainstorm over ways to create new phone lists, compile the list and make the calls. I used to track down phone numbers for people listed in the morning newspaper under the Incorporation Notices and make a call to them in an attempt to sell them a pension plan. It was a good idea in theory but yielded poor results. None of the companies I contacted had an interest in me or the fact I had a Series 7 license.

The phone I was using might have been broken. It only worked for me when I was making outbound calls. None of the people I left messages for called me. Nobody heard through the grapevine that I was selling investments and called me out of the blue to discuss the best way to invest the fresh inheritance they had just received or their lottery winnings. The phone only rang for me a few times, but those calls were never from potential clients. The only people who called me were wholesalers who worked for mutual fund companies. My company had given them my name. Because I was a new broker, the wholesalers wanted to get me interested in their mutual funds as early as possible. When they called, it was always with an invitation to lunch. Being a person with a great appetite, I never declined. The lunches I and the other new brokers were taken to were always first rate, and the food was exceptional. I don't remember much about the sales pitches given to me by the wholesalers, but I remember the food. To this day, the only reason I was in certain high class restaurants in Pittsburgh was because a mutual fund wholesaler took me there.

What was tough about my new career was that the job I left supplied me with a lot of responsibility and authority. People were constantly calling me offering me real estate deals, loan proposals and investment opportunities for my boss. When I called somebody, they called me back. I traveled, I approved or disapproved transactions, I met with investment bankers, and I had a great time. Sitting at the tin desk making calls on a telephone that didn't ring was not cutting it. Less than two months after obtaining my license I contemplated leaving the investment business.

What made me decide to actually leave was something that happened with the wife of the owner of the business. She was an attractive woman in her early 30's. Her husband was in his 50's, and my first impression when I met them was they were actually father and daughter. Before I realized they were married, I had already made plans on how I was going to ask her out. She was the driver of the Porsche 944 that sat in the front of the parking lot that had motivated me to walk into the building. This woman was always well-dressed and got many of her clients through referrals and through the social and religious organizations she belonged to.

At the time I was sitting at my desk trying to get somebody on the phone to talk to me, limited partnerships that offered investments into cable-TV were being sold by investment brokers. The history behind this investment is as follows: in the early 1980's, most cable television systems owned in the country were owned and operated by 'Mom & Pop' type of operators. The industry was still regulated and the big Multiple System Operators had not yet gotten into the business. Consumers were still looking at cable as a way to get better reception and the popular cable networks of today had not yet launched. Syndicators of cable partnerships were able to buy systems at low prices, string together neighboring systems to form larger systems, and increase penetration rates and monthly fees by adding more programming and subscribers. In short, the syndicators were able to increase the value of the systems they were purchasing. Investors were willing to supply the syndicators with the capital they needed because it was a 'buyer's market' and there was upside potential for their money.

By the middle of the decade, things had changed dramatically. The business was about to be deregulated, the launching and growth of the cable networks was creating a demand among TV watchers and the companies that were to become the largest operators, (TCI, Time, Warner, Cablevision, etc.) had gotten into the business, and they were buying up systems. Their cost of capital was much lower than that required by equity investors in limited partnerships. The prices Mom & Pop were getting for their systems went from about $200.00 per subscriber in the early 1980's to $600.00 per subscriber in the mid- to late 1980's. A 'buyer's market' had become a 'seller's market' and Mom & Pop were glad of that fact as they collected bigger and bigger checks from the sale of their systems.

But Mom & Pop's good fortune was to the detriment of the syndicators and their limited partnerships. The way they bought systems in the early 1980's could no longer be done. There was too much competition for systems and too many well financed companies looking to buy those systems.

There was one syndicator in particular who had built a nice portfolio of cable systems when the pickings were ripe. Some of their early partnerships had gone full cycle, and the investors received tax deductions, their initial capital plus a sizable return on their investment. But as the tide changed in the industry...as the number of buyers increased...it was hard for a syndicator to find an undervalued system, increase the number of channels and number of subscribers and sell it for twice the price in five years. A major tax law change in 1986 decreased the advantages of investing in limited partnerships.

The only way this syndicator could raise money was by having investment brokers sell partnership interests to their clients. With the increased competition for cable systems and the lack of tax benefits, the company was having trouble raising money. Instead of realizing that the market and tax law changes meant they would need to develop a new business plan, they did what many syndicators did as a way to entice brokers to push their product...they organized a sales contest.

The contest was already underway when I got into the business.

The broker who sold the most cable-TV partnership units over a certain time period would receive an all-expenses paid trip to Rio Di Janeiro. *(Sales contests as a way to motivate brokers to sell a certain product have since been curtailed).* The contest was coming to a close at the same time I was sitting at the tin desk in the upstairs part of the building. The wife of the owner was in third place, behind a broker in Denver and one in New York City.

As the deadline approached, the owner's wife was given an introduction to a group of nuns who lived in a small convent in the Pittsburgh area. The nuns had $200,000 in assets and were interested in investing their money. You can probably write the remainder of this chapter. In order to go from third place to first place, in order to win the trip to Rio, the owner's wife ended putting a sizable percentage of the nuns' money into a cable-TV limited partnership. In the past when I've told this story I've been asked how the cable investment turned out. People wanted to know if the nuns made any money.

The answer to that question is this: If you, the reader of this book, asked that question to yourself while reading the preceding paragraphs, you don't understand one of the most important fundamental concepts of the investment business. And beginning in the next section you will learn that concept along with everything else you need to learn about proper investment analysis.

It was a combination of things, not just the nuns' getting stuck with a cable-TV investment, that made me give up my tin desk and have my license placed in escrow by the NASD. My career as an investment broker was short but certainly not sweet.

We fear things in proportion to our ignorance of them.

—Livy (Roman historian; 59 B.C. - 17 A.D.)

I am an expert on the history and mechanics of the stock market, on proper asset allocation, how to choose an asset manager and numerous minute details of proper investment analysis. I know how to separate valid and relevant investment information from invalid and insignificant information constantly being supplied by investment sales people, by your friends who think they know about the investment business, and by the media.

I do not know much about computers (including the computer I am writing this book on), carpentry (even though I have done construction work) or cars (even though I used to work in a gas station). I deal with a variety of people with differing levels of education and from many different professions. Some are business owners, some are white collar employees of large and small corporations, and some are blue collar workers. I appreciate their professions, their hard work and the skill used in their crafts and trades. But I also appreciate this fact: regardless of who they are, what they do, or their level of schooling, the people I deal with do not understand the basic mechanics of proper investment analysis. Does that statement sound a bit harsh? Well, read on. Many people who work in the investment business do not understand the true mechanics of the stock market, the related ancillary facts that determine success or failure in investing and the specifics of structuring an investment portfolio.

Now, go back and reread the quote at the beginning of this chapter. A number of people who just read that quote are afraid of investments and investment salespeople. Once again, the range of people who are afraid encompasses highly educated people, physicians, business owners, pension plan sponsors, craftsmen, educators, laborers, butchers, bakers, candlestick makers and any other occupation you can imagine. Their fear is a direct result of their lack of knowledge. And guess what? I used to be afraid of the investment business and investment selection. I wasn't sure that what I was telling people during that time period when I was sitting upstairs at my tin desk making phone calls was relevant or not. I didn't know if the dialogue that comprised my sales pitch had any significance. I'm embarrassed to say that some of the things I said were told to me by the mutual fund wholesalers over the expensive lunches they treated me to, and I simply repeated it to prospective customers.

I am no longer afraid of any aspect of the investment business. I now have total knowledge of, and clear insight into, each aspect of the business. I know how to separate the diversionary spiel and hype associated with a sales pitch from the important, meaningful and pertinent factual information that one needs in order to function in and around the world of investments and with people in the investment business. Jim Morrison, the long since departed lead singer of The Doors, once said "Face your fears and they will become your strength." I faced my fears and now know every fundamental aspect of the investment business. This knowledge is part of my strength. And I am going to give you the knowledge...and the strength...I have acquired. Before I do that, however, I must get you back on track with my journey through the investment business because how I obtained that knowledge is as important as the knowledge itself.

After I gave up my tin desk at the investment company, I put my Series 7 license in escrow with the NASD. My partner in the fledgling cable-TV system became my ex-partner as we sold the only private system we operated. My share of the proceeds was small but enough to keep my bills paid until I started to generate other income. I did that by going back to work for my old boss and working on projects that had me once again traveling, this time to both Florida and California. Most of the projects were connected to the real estate and banking industries, and although my level of ability in both arenas is top notch, I knew I didn't want to make a career out of either. While working in the city of Gainesville, Florida, on an extended assignment in 1991, I met a girl who was studying gerontology at the University of Florida. I always had an interest in the subject of aging and preventive health and, while still in Florida, began a self-study project that applied the techniques of economic analysis and investment research to the areas of nutrition, fitness, lifestyle factors and the business of medicine. That self-study project has since turned into a passion and business venture that combines my interest in preventive health with my ability to find value in information and products being marketed or supplied by the healthcare industry.

My investment license came out of escrow a couple of times and was placed with a Broker/Dealer to keep it in good standing with the NASD. The majority of my work time was spent on real estate projects for my former employer.

Around 1995 things changed for me regarding the investment business. I became aware of an investment vehicle known as Low Income Housing Tax Credits. This program was born with the implementation of IRS Code Section 42, a part of the Tax Reform Act of 1986. Before 1986 investors were able to reduce their tax liability by investing in real estate tax shelters that created a paper loss for investors. These paper losses were deducted from a taxpayer's ordinary income and lowered an investor's tax liability. The only problem was that many of the real estate projects had no economic value;there was a glut of empty office buildings and shopping centers, and older investors were being taken advantage of by brokers in search of the high commissions that these types of products generated (similar to cable-TV limited partnerships). Congress wanted to eliminate these so-called 'abusive tax shelters' and regain the tax revenue being lost. They did this by implementing rules that required an investor in a tax-advantaged investment to be able to deduct losses from "passive" activities only from income that was derived from other "passive" activities...meaning the investor had to have no management responsibility in the investment or no liability beyond that of their initial investment.

The passive loss rules effectively shut down the real estate tax shelter industry overnight. Congress had solved the problem of abusive tax shelters (although the problems created by the abusive partnerships linger on to this day). But Congress had another problem.

That problem was the need for quality affordable housing. At the time the new rules went into effect, it was estimated that there was a demand for over 5 million affordable housing units (by definition, affordable housing is a unit rented to a family whose income level is at or below 60% of the corresponding county's median income and where the tenant pays no more than 30% of their household income for rent).

Picture in your mind what the housing defined as 'public housing' looks like. This is what served as affordable housing before 1986. The institutional-like, non-descript, drab buildings that provided little or no hope for the residents who 'existed' in the buildings instead of 'lived' there were our country's answer to the problem of providing low-income families with a quality place to live.

At the same time the tax shelter industry was shut down, Congress also developed a way to get the government out of the business of building and managing low-income housing and getting the private sector into the business. In 1986, Congress created Section 42 of the IRS Code. This part of the IRS Code provided federal Tax Credits for individuals and corporations that invested in the development and management of low-income housing. Instead of receiving cash flow from the ownership of real estate, investors would receive the right to reduce their tax liability. The plan was to get the government, which is inefficient by nature, out of the housing business and get the private sector, with its corresponding efficiencies, into the business. Anybody who has ever complained about too much government would have to appreciate this program.

I became aware of Section 42 Tax Credits when I was still working for my ex-boss and developing my preventive healthcare company. When I heard about Tax Credits I decided to reinstate my broker's license and specialize in educating investors about the mechanics and value of the Credits and selling them investments that provided ownership in affordable housing.

I found a syndicator, Boston Capital, that had been developing low-income housing under the old rules before the Tax Credit program started. They had focused their efforts on building and managing low-income housing under the new tax rules and had built a spectacular track record in bringing the finished product to the market. My license was placed with a new Broker/Dealer and I hit the pavement trying to simultaneously teach investors about Tax Credits and sell them an investment into a Boston Capital low-income housing program.

My marketing effort began by contacting the largest CPA firms in town and trying to get the attention of the accountant in charge of tax preparation for clients. Much to my surprise and disappointment, the accountants I talked to, or attempted to talk to, were apathetic about Section 42 Tax Credits. Some CPA's I met dismissed the Credits outright because they had not heard of them. Other CPA's did not believe that Credits were an actual part of the IRS Code. One CPA, who happened to work for one of the Big Five (at the time Big Seven) firms, got into an argument with me over whether or not Section 42 was an actual part of the Code or a "loophole based on a loose interpretation of the Code." It was this gentleman's ignorance that steered me to the State Board of Accountancy where I became certified to teach accountants and provide them with Professional Continuing Education credits *(the obvious joke here is that it is difficult to teach anything to a group of people who feel they already know everything)*.

My marketing effort continued. I had two articles published locally about the history, mechanics, and value of Tax Credits. I made two appearances on radio shows and one appearance on a business TV show to talk about the Credit program. A direct mail campaign and cable-TV commercials followed.

Unfortunately, my interest and enthusiasm for low-income housing Tax Credits was not shared with CPA's or the investing public. By the time I was aggressively marketing the product, the Credits had been part of the IRS Code for 9 years. Either I overestimated my ability to teach people why there was value in the program or investors just didn't care. Except for one of my ex-accounting instructors at Duquesne University who bought Credits and referred some clients to me, and a few older, high income individuals who used the Credits to offset their tax liability, I didn't crash the marketplace as I thought I would. My efforts failed. The time I spent marketing to accountants was wasted. The money I spent on my TV commercial and the cost of the air time was a bad investment on my part. (The majority of the money was spent on the air time. The commercial itself only cost $86.00 to produce). At the time I realized I was not going to make a living selling low-income housing Tax Credits, I had a thought that if someone were to study my experience in the investment business they would come to the conclusion that I was a failure. My cash flow was so poor that I almost simultaneously became an expert on Low Income Housing and a resident of the same.

And it was precisely at this point that this story really and truly begins.

When I was at the point where I realized I wouldn't be selling Credits I was up against the wall. I had a NASD Series 7 license in good standing and no clients. I was legally able to sell stocks, bonds, mutual funds, options, and limited partnerships and to open margin accounts, but I didn't know many people who could use these products, and I didn't know how to find them. In addition, I didn't know enough about these products or the investment business to talk intelligently about them. I had no confidence in my knowledge of investments. In short, I was afraid.

It was at this time that I took Jim Morrison's advice and faced my fears. I used my training in economics and my experience performing investment research to start from ground zero. I became totally objective about the business, about investment products and about other brokers. I focused on finding the best way to determine what investment information was relevant and important and what information was part of the sales process or part of the diversionary process and being used to hide the valid data and/or facts. In Part Two of this book I am going to share the findings of my research with you. One of the most ironic items in my life is the fact that almost every significant bit of information I have learned about investing money and my insight into the true workings of the investment business came into my grasp after I obtained my license to sell investments. And you are about to learn those very same things.

PART

TWO

The key to genius is simplicity.

—Francis Albert Sinatra (1915-1998)

I n preparing to write this manuscript I made a visit to a bookstore. The business section was populated with investment-related books that could be divided into two types. The first type of book offered advice on how to become rich investing in stocks during any market condition using some secret technique that the author perfected. The titles were sexy and promised much more than the contents of the book could ever deliver. The second type of book was yet another attempt to teach the reader the basics of investing. The advice in the first type of book is usually not worth the price paid for the information and the second type of book is a rehash of basic concepts that investors have been unable to grasp from previous books. The first type of book outnumbered the second type by a 4 to 1 margin.

The purpose of this book is to teach the reader not to waste time or money on the first type of book and to make the second type unnecessary. I will teach you...in a simple yet insightful manner...what you need to know about the investment business so that you are not afraid of dealing with money issues or dealing with people in the industry. This is the most relevant and factual investment book you will ever read. If you read any others from this point on, they will serve as reinforcement to what you are about to learn and also as a reminder as to how much invalid, hyped and misleading information is peddled to you every day by the publishing industry. This is the very reason I continue to read newly published investment-related books.

Listed below are ten sections that will provide detailed and insightful information into what really matters about investing. When you read and digest the information in these sections, you will have more knowledge of investment analysis than many people working in the business. The order of information is as important as the information itself as each section provides a foundation for what follows.

The Ten Sections are:

    I. *History and Mechanics of the Capital Markets*
   II. *Impact of Inflation on Investing*
  III. *How Stocks are Valued*
  IV. *Why Stocks are Your Best Investment*
   V. *The Proper Way to Buy and Own Stocks*
  VI. *The Cost to Buy Stocks vs. The Cost to Own Stocks*
 VII. *Portfolio Turnover Rates—What You Make vs. What You Keep*
VIII. *Asset Allocation—Avoiding a 'Pain in the Assets'*
  IX. *Dealing With the Media—How to Separate News From Stuff Put In to Create More Space Between the Ads*
   X. *Putting It All Together—The 'MTV' Approach to Investing.*

Enjoy the Ten Sections. By the time you reach the end of Part Two your knowledge of the investment business will have increased substantially.

I. History and Mechanics of the Capital Markets

T he term 'capital markets' is used to describe the combined stock markets, bond markets and interest-bearing instruments offered by banks and savings institutions. This is the investment universe we will be studying. A proper foundation for your understanding of investment analysis and portfolio structure is a working knowledge of the historic average yields, ranges and fluctuations of each category. Before we begin our study I want to go off on a brief tangent.

I am always asked what the 'best investment' is. Before I provide the information you are about to review I would like to preface my answer by stating that the 'best investment' may be an investment in yourself. Money spent on meaningful educational pursuits could have a Rate of Return that would be impossible to measure. The value of the house you live in and raise your family in cannot truly be measured using any of the tools we use in financial ratio analysis. Any additions you make to your house to make it more comfortable or that bring you inner peace and tranquility are off the scale when we try to perform an Internal Rate of Return. And how do we measure the yield on an investment consisting of your finances, time, creativity and passion molded into your own well-researched and well-managed business? Especially if those efforts provide a product or service that has high demand? That type of investment provides returns that will put you in the neighborhood of infinity once you factor in the feelings of achievement, accomplishment and self-worth that owning your own business provides.

The 'best investment?' I don't know exactly what the answer to that question is. What I do know is everything that you need to know about stocks, bonds, and bank accounts, and that is what you are about to learn.

When the term 'stock market' is used today it actually is used to describe numerous markets. In addition to the large company U.S. market (what is being described when people talk about "The Dow" or the "S&P 500"), there are also technology/biotechnology stocks (often times used to describe many of the issues on the NASDAQ market), mid-sized company stocks, small company stocks, international stocks issued by companies in both developed and developing countries and markets that are specific to a certain industry, also known as sectors.

For the purpose of gauging performance and making comparisons, we use various indexes. With the explosion of the various markets came a corresponding explosion in the number of indexes. An index is a tool used to measure the performance of a particular investment vehicle against vehicles with a similar objective. There may be over 200 various indexes if the numerous subsectors and individual country indexes are taken into account. For the purposes of this project the domestic stock market index we will study will be the Standard & Poor's 500 Composite Index (S&P 500). This index provides a broader, more reflective view of the American economy than the better known 30-company Dow Jones Industrial Average. For international stocks we will be studying the EAFE (Europe, Australia, Far East) Index. For corporate and government bond yields we will use data compiled by the investment advisory services firm, Ibbotson Associates. Their tabulation takes into account various relevant parameters that determine a bond's return (coupon rate, interest rate changes, the inflation rate, default rate, investment grade) to determine an Average Annual Return. The return on bank savings accounts comes from the U.S. League of Savings Institutions (now known as America's Community Bankers) and reflects the yields on various deposit instruments. The Consumer Price Index is monitored by the Bureau of Labor Statistics and reflects price changes in a specific listing of goods and services. The S&P Index, long-term corporate and government bonds, and CPI are supplied from 1950 through 2000. The EAFE Index is supplied from 1970 (its year of inception) until 2000. Savings account information is supplied from 1950 through 1999. The figure for Year 2000 was not available. The yields for each category are presented for your review in Tables 1 through 6. Please review each table and return to this point of the text.

Table 7 provides the following information for each category: average yield, the value at the end of 2000 of $1.00 invested in each category in 1950 (for the CPI we are showing the cost, in Year 2000, of items that $1.00 could purchase in 1950;for the EAFE index we calculated the result over a 51-year period using the results from the 31-year lifetime of this index), the number of positive and negative years for each category and the Standard Deviation of each category except for the CPI. Standard Deviation is defined as the average difference from the average for a listing of data. This statistical device is used to measure the volatility of a group of numbers. Related notes to the data are also supplied in Table 7. Please review Table 7 and then return to the text.

Here is what you need to learn from the historical data: the highest average returns of the investment categories are found in the domestic and international stock markets. The average returns were substantially higher than the returns from bonds. The higher average return was achieved even though the stock market indexes had negative returns in significant percentages of the study periods (11 years or 21% of the time for the S&P 500 and 8 years or 25% of the time for the EAFE). These negative years accounted for the higher Standard Deviations (17.76 for the S&P 500 and 22.87 for the EAFE). This is one fact of investment life that you must become comfortable with: stock markets decline in price approximately one out of every 4 to 5 years. The return, or reward, for realizing this is an Average Annual Return (AAR) far in excess of other types of investment vehicles. The rewards for understanding this are often provided in the years immediately following the year of the market decline. As evidence: the AAR for the S&P 500 in the years after a negative year has been 21.51% and 16.48% for the EAFE *(these yields take into account the decline in value from the years of consecutive market declines for both indexes but not the results for the year after the market decline that occurred in the year 2000).*

The low returns from corporate and government bonds and bank savings instruments are associated with a lower Standard Deviation. You 'pay' for the lower volatility by accepting a lower return. The yield is further reduced by the guarantees associated with government bonds and bank savings instruments. You pay even more for the guarantee by accepting a lower yield.

You will notice that the bond categories had more years of negative returns (14 for the corporate bond index and 17 for the government bond index) than the stock indexes. This result occurred because the value of a bond index will decrease any year in which there is a rise in interest rates. Higher interest rates attached to newly issued bonds make the value of existing bonds decline. There is an inverse relationship between the value of a bond and change in interest rates. During the periods 1978 through 1981 and 1977 through 1980 the corporate bond index and the government bond index, respectively, posted consecutive annual negative returns. The relatively high Standard Deviation for both bond categories shows that there is excessive volatility associated with a low AAR.

The last item you need to learn from the information presented is the concept and power of 'compounded growth.' Take another look at the value of $1.00 invested in 1950 and allowed to grow until the end of Year 2000. The returns from the stock indexes trounce any other return and the bond/bank returns did not fare much better than the CPI. (Another way of looking at the CPI factor is to state that the general cost of living increased 7.5 times during the 51-year period under study. Section II will provide more detail into the impact of inflation on your investment dollars.)

John D. Rockefeller referred to compounded growth as "the eighth wonder of the world" and you can see why from the results in Table 7. Here's another concept for you: 'The Rule of 72.' This edict states that the result of dividing the number 72 by the yield of an investment provides the number of years it will take for that investment to double. As an example, the AAR of the S&P 500 Index was 14.32% for 51 years.

If your investment earns this rate, it will take 5.02 years for your money to double. If you earn the average rate on money invested in corporate bonds, it will take 11.09 years for your money to double.

Compounded growth is so powerful that even a modest difference in rates of return will result in huge differences in account valuations. Listed below are the 5, 10, 15 and 20 year valuations for two portfolios. Both portfolios have $10,000 at the beginning of the study period. Portfolio A earns 10% per year and Portfolio B earns 12% per year.

	Portfolio A	Portfolio B	% Difference
Year 5	$16,105	$17,623	9.4%
Year 10	$25,937	$31,058	19.74%
Year 15	$41,772	$54,735	31.0%
Year 20	$67,275	$96,462	43.38%

A relatively small, 2%, difference in annual yields results in a growing disparity in the value of the accounts. In Section VIII you will learn about the importance of asset allocation and why not understanding what you've learned in this Section can cost you a tremendous amount of money.

Table 1.   S&P 500 Composite Index
Annual Returns 1950-2000

Year	Return %	Year	Return %	Year	Return %
1950	31.46	1968	11.04	1986	18.62
1951	23.97	1969	(8.04)	1987	5.18
1952	18.16	1970	3.89	1988	16.50
1953	(0.94)	1971	14.22	1989	31.59
1954	52.27	1972	18.96	1990	(3.11)
1955	31.41	1973	(14.67)	1991	30.34
1956	6.48	1974	(26.31)	1992	7.61
1957	(10.72)	1975	37.14	1993	10.03
1958	43.15	1976	23.81	1994	1.36
1959	11.95	1977	(7.19)	1995	37.44
1960	0.45	1978	6.52	1996	22.90
1961	26.88	1979	18.45	1997	33.32
1962	(8.66)	1980	32.45	1998	28.52
1963	22.76	1981	(4.88)	1999	21.01
1964	16.43	1982	21.50	2000	(9.11)
1965	12.46	1983	22.46		
1966	(10.02)	1984	6.22		
1967	23.89	1985	31.64		

Source: Ibbotson Associates

Table 2.   EAFE Index
Annual Returns 1970-2000

Year	Return %	Year	Return %	Year	Return %
1970	(10.51)	1981	(1.03)	1992	(11.85)
1971	31.21	1982	(0.86)	1993	32.94
1972	37.60	1983	24.61	1994	8.06
1973	(14.17)	1984	7.86	1995	11.55
1974	(22.15)	1985	56.72	1996	6.36
1975	37.10	1986	69.94	1997	2.06
1976	3.74	1987	24.93	1998	20.33
1977	19.42	1988	28.59	1999	27.30
1978	34.30	1989	10.80	2000	(13.96)
1979	6.18	1990	(23.20)		
1980	24.43	1991	12.50		

Source: Ibbotson Associates

Table 3.   Long Term Corporate Bond
Annual Returns 1950-2000

Year	Return %	Year	Return %	Year	Return %
1950	2.12	1968	2.57	1986	19.85
1951	(2.69)	1969	(8.09)	1987	(0.27)
1952	3.52	1970	18.37	1988	10.70
1953	3.41	1971	11.01	1989	16.23
1954	5.39	1972	7.26	1990	6.78
1955	0.48	1973	1.14	1991	19.89
1956	(6.81)	1974	(3.06)	1992	9.39
1957	8.71	1975	14.64	1993	13.19
1958	(2.22)	1976	18.65	1994	(5.76)
1959	(0.97)	1977	1.71	1995	27.20
1960	9.07	1978	(.07)	1996	1.40
1961	4.82	1979	(4.18)	1997	12.95
1962	7.95	1980	(2.76)	1998	10.76
1963	2.19	1981	(1.24)	1999	(7.45)
1964	4.77	1982	42.56	2000	12.87
1965	0.46	1983	6.26		
1966	0.20	1984	16.86		
1967	(4.95)	1985	30.09		

Source: Ibbotson Associates

Table 4. Long Term Government Bonds Annual Returns 1950-2000

Year	Return %	Year	Return %	Year	Return %
1950	0.06	1968	(0.26)	1986	24.53
1951	(3.93)	1969	(5.07)	1987	(2.71)
1952	1.16	1970	12.11	1988	9.67
1953	3.64	1971	13.23	1989	18.11
1954	7.19	1972	5.69	1990	6.18
1955	(1.29)	1973	(1.11)	1991	19.30
1956	(5.59)	1974	4.35	1992	8.05
1957	7.46	1975	9.20	1993	18.24
1958	(6.09)	1976	16.75	1994	(7.77)
1959	(2.26)	1977	(0.69)	1995	31.67
1960	13.78	1978	(1.18)	1996	(0.93)
1961	0.97	1979	(1.23)	1997	15.85
1962	6.89	1980	(3.95)	1998	13.06
1963	1.21	1981	1.86	1999	(8.96)
1964	3.51	1982	40.36	2000	21.48
1965	0.71	1983	0.65		
1966	3.65	1984	15.48		
1967	(9.18)	1985	30.97		

Source: Ibbotson Associates

Table 5. Consumer Price Index 1950-2000

Year	Return %	Year	Return %	Year	Return %
1950	5.93	1968	4.72	1986	1.10
1951	6.00	1969	6.20	1987	4.43
1952	0.75	1970	5.57	1988	4.42
1953	0.75	1971	3.27	1989	4.65
1954	(0.74)	1972	3.41	1990	6.11
1955	0.37	1973	8.71	1991	3.06
1956	2.99	1974	12.34	1992	2.90
1957	2.90	1975	6.94	1993	2.75
1958	1.76	1976	4.86	1994	2.67
1959	1.73	1977	6.70	1995	2.54
1960	1.36	1978	9.02	1996	3.32
1961	0.67	1979	13.29	1997	1.70
1962	1.33	1980	12.52	1998	1.61
1963	1.64	1981	8.92	1999	2.68
1964	0.97	1982	3.83	2000	3.39
1965	1.92	1983	3.79		
1966	3.46	1984	3.95		
1967	3.04	1985	3.80		

Source: U.S. Bureau of Labor Statistics

Table 6.   Savings Account Returns 1950-2000

Year	Return %	Year	Return %	Year	Return %
1950	1.8	1968	4.7	1986	7.0
1951	1.9	1969	4.9	1987	5.5
1952	2.0	1970	5.1	1988	6.6
1953	2.1	1971	5.2	1989	7.3
1954	2.2	1972	5.2	1990	7.1
1955	2.3	1973	5.7	1991	6.3
1956	2.5	1974	6.4	1992	4.5
1957	2.8	1975	6.2	1993	3.6
1958	2.9	1976	6.1	1994	3.5
1959	3.1	1977	6.1	1995	4.5
1960	3.3	1978	6.4	1996	4.5
1961	3.4	1979	7.4	1997	4.6
1962	3.8	1980	8.9	1998	4.6
1963	3.9	1981	11.0	1999	4.6
1964	3.9	1982	10.9	2000	•
1965	4.1	1983	9.2		
1966	4.4	1984	9.6		
1967	4.6	1985	8.1		

• *This figure is no longer tabulated. If it were, the number would probably be lower than the 4.6% rate from 1997-1999.*

Source: U.S. League of Savings Institutions & Federal Reserve Board

Table 7.   Tabulation of Data—Tables 1-6

	AAR*	Value of $1.00 in 2000	+/- Years	Standard Deviation
S&P 500	14.32%	$920.94	40/11	17.76
EAFE	14.22%	$880.74	23/8	22.87
Corp Bonds	6.49%	$24.70	37/14	10.09
Gov't. Bonds	6.37%	$23.32	34/17	10.03
Savings Accts	5.12%	$12.80	51/0	2.24
CPI	4.03%	$7.50	50/1	n/a

*Average Annual Return

The following shows the AAR of each category if we remove the years with the highest and lowest yields. This is helpful because it will eliminate aberrations in the data. ( ) signifies a year with a negative return.

	Highest Year	Lowest Year	Adjusted AAR
S&P 500	52.27/1954	(26.31)/1974	14.37%
EAFE	69.94/1986	(23.20)/1990	13.58%
Corp Bonds	42.56/1982	(8.09)/1969	6.05%
Gov't Bonds	40.36/1982	(9.10)1967	5.99%
Savings Accts	11.00/1981	1.8/1950	5.06%
CPI	13.29/1979	(0.74)/1954	3.93%

Note that all adjusted investment categories had decreases in their AAR except for the S&P Index. The adjusted returns for the bond indexes decreased 0.44% and 0.38%, respectively.

II. The Impact of Inflation on Your Investments

One of the toughest tasks I face as an investment advisor is finding ways to teach investors about the biggest risk they face. There are many types of risks faced by investors (market risk, interest rate risk, ineffective management risk, fiscal policy risk, risks associated with technology change and/or failure, litigation risk, sector risk, credit risk, risk of nondiversification, risks associated with international investment and political change, etc). But the biggest risk investors face is the risk of losing their purchasing power because of increases in the inflation rate. The prices of most goods and services you utilize in your day-to-day existence increase constantly. If you are not invested properly, you will have a steady decline in the value of your assets and a weakening of your purchasing power.

Table 5 shows the annual change in the Consumer Price Index (CPI) from 1950 to 2000. The inflation rate has averaged 4.03% annually over the time period under study. There was only one year, 1954, when the CPI decreased instead of increased. And that deflation was minor (0.74%).

If we do a 'reverse Rule of 72' we will find that the cost of living, on average, doubles every 17.86 years. The real return of your investments has to be adjusted for the impact of inflation. The average 'real' return of the investment indexes from 1950 through 2000 is listed below:

S&P 500	14.32 - 4.03	=	10.29
EAFE	14.22 - 4.03	=	10.19
Corp Bonds	6.49 - 4.03	=	2.46
Gov't Bonds	6.37 - 4.03	=	2.34
Bank Acct	5.12 - 4.03	=	1.09

As I write this section I can look up at my office wall at a framed crisp $1.00 bill. This $1.00 was left to me by my grandfather who was the proprietor of a South Side pool room. When he died all 35 of his grandchildren were given $1.00 bills. My grandfather died in 1976. Because the dollar has been literally hanging around since I received it, the value of it has decreased each year. In terms of today's purchasing power, my dollar is worth only 29.45% of what it was when I received it in 1976. The real value of my dollar is the message it carries about the impact of inflation on purchasing power.

One of my biggest challenges in the investment business is teaching investors what the terms 'safe' and 'conservative' mean. People who think bonds and bank instruments are safe are not taking into consideration the negative impact of the CPI on their money. For a long term investor, bonds and CDs are definitely not safe. They are not without risk. The risk they bring is the greatest risk an investor faces: a decrease in their purchasing power. All the risks I listed at the beginning of this section can be minimized or eliminated with prudent research, proper asset manager selection and diversification. The risk of losing your purchasing power can only be overcome with a comfort level of the mechanics of stocks and proper asset allocation among the various stock markets.

One of the reasons you have to invest against the effects of inflation is the fact that you and your spouse will probably live longer than your parents and previous generations. The more years you live, the more of a risk you face in losing your purchasing power or even outliving your assets. The U.S. Census Bureau reports that the number of people over the age of 65 increased from 16.6 million to 34.9 million between 1960 and 2000. The number of people over age 65 is projected to be 56.2 million by the year 2020. The percentage of the population over age 65 will be 16.5% by 2020 compared to 9.2% in 1960. The number of Americans over age 85 is expected to increase from 900,000 in 1960 to 7.3 million by 2020. A newborn today has a life expectancy in excess of 76 years. A person who turns 70 this year is expected to live an additional 16 years.

If your investments are only keeping pace with, or barely beating, increases in the annual cost of living, your living standard will struggle to stay even with the lifestyle you are used to. Beyond that, if the bond and bank instruments you have your assets invested in are in a non-deferred account (not in a 401(k), IRA or variable annuity account) the yield is reduced further by the income taxes you must pay on the interest income you receive. It was once stated to me that the yield you receive on a bank Certificate of Deposit is roughly equal to the cost of living plus the income tax rate. Subtract those two items from your yield and your real return is zero or below zero. Investments with low yields are not giving you a chance to take advantage of compounded growth and not allowing your money to work for you as hard as you work for your money.

Here's more bad news about inflation *(don't worry;we'll end this section with good news about inflation)*. While the CPI index has averaged 4.03% for 51 years, certain segments of the economy have had inflation rates higher than the CPI. Two perfect examples come from two areas that affect most of the people reading this book. Those areas are medical care and tuition. While the CPI averaged 3.36% during the 11-year period from 1990-2000, the inflation rates in the medical industry and for education purposes were much higher. Medical costs rose on average 6.45% each year and the cost of higher education increased 8.63%. Let's put these percentage increases into numbers for a direct comparison. The goods and services that cost you $1,000.00 in 1990 cost you $1,379.70 in year 2000. Medical care that cost you $1,000.00 in 1990 cost you $1,713.20 in 2000. Education expenses of $1,000.00 in 1990 would have cost you $1,950.00 in 2000. The cost of getting educated in the 1990's basically doubled. This followed the decade of the 1980's in which medical care inflation was double that of the overall inflation rate, and the prices of pharmaceuticals increased three times faster than the general inflation rate. *(I just had a flashback to my first semester at Community College. My per credit cost was $19.00. The per credit cost at Community College today is $68.00—a 257% total increase or a 6% annual increase).*

Do you think you will have to pay medical costs in the future? Do you have your children's tuition payments to look forward to? Of course you do. Except for an extremely limited number of items that will have a price reduction because of technology changes, production economies or increased competition, most things you need to spend money on (products, taxes, insurance coverages, utility expenses, food, transportation, services...the list is inclusive of almost everything) will cost more in the future than they do right now. So let me hammer the point again. If you have your assets invested in investment categories that only keep pace with inflation (or dip below it after you pay taxes) your standard of living will be negatively impacted. You will be limited in your purchases. You will have to do without. You will not have a legacy to leave to your children and your grandchildren.

You may have something else to look forward to. Because of the changes in demographics among Americans you may find yourself in the position where you are providing care for an elderly adult and a young child, teenager or young adult who hasn't finished his/her education or been able to establish his/her own income and residence. You may have financial commitments to the generation before you and after you at the same time. The chances are that your money will be spent on tuition and medical care on both ends.

Now here is the promised good news about the inflation rate and it is something I learned from my study of medical economics. The average inflation rate of 4.03% was arrived at over the last 51 years. The range of those years was (.74%) to 13.29%. The average was highly influenced by the increased inflation rate that affected our economy during the 13-year period 1969-1981. During that period the inflation rate averaged a staggering 7.82% with the highest rates occurring in 1979 (13.29%), 1980 (12.52%) and 1974 (12.34%). Please note that during that time period the S&P 500 Index had an Average Annual Return of 7.25% and there were 5 years (38% of the time) with negative returns.

It doesn't take a Federal Reserve Board member to see that there is a positive correlation between an extended period of high inflation and low stock market returns. The reason for the correlation is that during periods of high inflation businesses have a hard time making money from their core business. The difficulty comes in the form of a doubleheader. Businesses find the high cost of borrowing a deterrent to investments in factories, inventory, labor, etc., and their lack of corporate investment creates a continued stagnation in corporate spending. Individuals find the high cost of borrowing a deterrent to acquiring new houses, remodeling existing homes, buying new or used cars or making any other large purchase that requires credit. A vicious cycle begins when the demand side of our economy (the consumer) stays quiet. The decrease in consumption keeps the supply side of our economy (plants, factories, etc.) quiet as well.

What happened to cause the aberration in the inflation rate between 1969 and 1981 combines politics, business, medicine, and the social sciences. In 1965 President Lyndon Johnson began the Great Society by simultaneously initiating the Medicare/Medicaid program and launching the 'War on Poverty.' To finance these programs Congress increased government spending substantially without raising income/corporate taxes or reducing other government spending (remember: the Vietnam War was also heating up and needed to be financed). The government printing presses started printing dollars to pay for the increased medical coverage, welfare, housing and educational programs. The immediate effects were all positive--people got healthcare, housing, job training, etc. But the longer term effects were negative. The creating of new dollars made the value of the existing dollars in the marketplace worth less. The amount of dollars circulating in the economy increased without a corresponding increase in productivity. More dollars chasing the same amount of goods and services will always lead to an increase in pricing of those goods and services. Just like my grandfather's dollar hanging on the wall, the value of each dollar was diminished.

The method used to finance Medicare/Medicaid, the War on Poverty and the war in Vietnam created an upward pressure on prices and resulted in the period of higher inflation that began in 1969. The end result was the dismal performance of the domestic stock market over that time period. *(The EAFE Index had an Average Annual Return of 12.17% from its inception in 1970 through the end of 1981. This result shows the importance of diversification and the value of investing in international stock markets.)*

Don't worry. The good news is still ahead.

How did we end the high inflation rate and get businesses and consumers to start investing and spending again? The person who slayed the inflation dragon was named Paul Volcker. Mr. Volcker was appointed by Jimmy Carter in 1979 to head the Federal Reserve Board and came into his office with a strong realization of the problem in the economy. Volcker reduced the growth of the money supply to a manageable 6% per year. By 1982 the CPI was reduced to 3.83% after posting rates of 13.29%, 12.52% and 8.92% between 1979 and 1981. Although Mr. Volcker was appointed by President Carter, the presidents who benefitted from his wise fiscal policy were Reagan and Clinton and everyone to follow. The halt to the runaway inflation is comparable to driving a car with faulty brakes down a steep hill. You pump the brakes and know you are going to be able to stop...you just don't know exactly when. Jimmy Carter started to apply the brakes, with the assistance of Paul Volcker;but it was Ronald Reagan sitting in the driver's seat when the car stopped. Mr. Volcker resigned from his position due to family and political pressures, even though the job is supposed to be totally absent of any and all politics. He resigned by declining to be considered for a third term as Federal Reserve Chairman. President Reagan appointed Alan Greenspan in 1987. Among the uninformed, Mr. Volcker gets little credit for the difficult situation he faced and how he handled it.

So where's the good news? Here it is: the Federal Reserve and Congress have learned the painful lesson about inflation. They will not allow the money supply to grow at the rate it did in the late 1960's and 1970's. Any increases in government spending will be done through an increase in taxes and/or a decrease in spending on other government programs. We will not have the high inflation rates that we had between 1969 and 1981. We will not have an extended period of inflation that results in an extended period of stock market returns substantially below the average.

One caveat: based on my knowledge of medical economics I cannot deliver any happy news about medical/pharmaceutical inflation. Those costs will most likely continue to rise at a rate in excess of the CPI. *If you wish to read a book that addresses this subject I suggest you read "The Medical-Industrial Complex" by Stanley M. Wohl, M.D. This book provides insightful detail on how the implementation of Medicare/Medicaid brought the corporate entity into the medical industry and created the incredible price increases associated with healthcare. The book was published back in 1984 but some of Dr. Wohl's predictions about the future (our present time) of the medical industry have become medical realities. One final note: when Medicare was started in 1965 it was estimated that by 1995 the government would be spending $9 billion per year on the program. The actual dollar amount spent in 1995 was $316 billion or 35 times more than the estimate.*

So much for estimates.

As for tuition inflation there isn't anything on the horizon to give hope to a slow down in the annual increases faced by students. My journey through college which featured a detour through Community College is a route that will be taken by more people...at the suggestion of their parents...in the future.

There is even more good news about inflation. While we most likely will not have high inflationary periods again (with the related periods of dismal stock market performance) our economy will still be subject to the business cycle. We will still have years of negative stock market returns. But not to worry. The overall return of stocks will soundly beat the other investment alternatives. Bond yields will decrease as overall interest rates stay closer to the 51-year average of 4.03% than the 1969-1981 average of 7.84% and bank instruments will be even lower. (If we subtract the 13-year return of the S&P Index of 7.25% during the 1969-1982 period, the index would have had an average annual return of 16.36% for the last half century).

My second piece of good news comes from a revelation I received while preparing the outline for this book. We will have years in which the inflation rate is positive but the stock market has a negative return. Because the inflation rate is reflected by an increase in the prices of goods and services in the economy, these increases will be reflected by an increase in the revenue and net income of the corporations whose stock you are invested in. This CPI increase is "owed" to the stock market each year that the market is negative and the inflation rate is positive. Refer back to Section I. The average annual return of the S&P 500 in the year following a negative year since 1950 is 21.51%. Part of that high return comes from the inflation rate that occurred during the year the market was negative. The fact that the stock market has a negative year presents a buying opportunity for investors, including the companies whose stocks have declined in price. By buying their own shares at a reduced price they are increasing the value of all other shares.

One last note on this subject--in any given year the chance that the cost of living will increase is **400%** greater than the stock market finishing that given year with a negative return.

I want to end this chapter with one final thought. I know there are many individuals who go to their job each day and work hard either physically, mentally or both. I also know there are many hard working entrepreneurs who are devoted to running their companies. It is always a source of disappointment to me when these hard-working people do not give their money a chance to work as hard as they do. Too much individual and 401(k)/Profit-sharing plan money is in non-growth investments when the purpose of the money is for living expenses during the account owner's retirement years. I hope some of the people have read to this point and will now realize that stocks have historically been the best investment and will be even a better investment into the future.

If you have been able to digest what I've written to this point you will see that investments in stocks have historically provided the highest returns for investors. The yield spread between stocks and other investments under study will be even greater in the future. Bonds and bank investments will be for only two types of people: the uninformed and those people parking their money for a short time.

Sections III and IV will provide you with more insight into the pricing of stocks and why stocks are your best investment choice.

III. How Stocks are Valued

There is a major difference between the **VALUE** of a stock and the **PRICE** of a stock. There are only two relevant things that determine a stock's value and there are many things, mostly irrelevant, that can determine the price.

A stock's value is determined by:

- The net income of the company issuing the stock.

- The prudent anticipation and potential of the company to increase its net income or begin generating net income at a foreseeable point in the future.

The concept of Price-Earnings Ratios is something that you should become familiar and comfortable with. It's an indication of what multiple of a company's per share earnings a prudent investor is willing to pay for a share of stock. The average P-E ratio of the S&P 500 covering the 75-year period from 1926 to 2000 has been 14. This means if a company was making $2.00 per share the market historically has been willing to apply a value of $28.00 per share to the stock of that company.

The P-E multiple investors are willing to accept today, under most circumstances, is around 20. For companies that are already profitable and are increasing their revenue, investors are willing to value the stock with a P-E ratio of approximately 30. If a company is making $2.00 of net income per share and is growing its revenue base, this company may be fairly priced at $60.00 per share. There are reasons why investors are willing to pay more for some stocks with a higher P-E ratio today than in the past. The reasons are legitimate and listed below:

- Investors have learned to live with the volatility of stocks and now realize that volatility is not the investor's enemy but their ally.

- The high inflation rate of the 1970's has been decreased to a level that will not negatively impact the long-term trend of the stock market.

- The yields on competitive investments will only mirror the inflation rate and investors have been educated to this fact.

- The huge increase in defined contribution plans such as 401(k) plans has developed a consistent stream of money being invested into stocks.

- The increase in popularity of mutual funds as a way to invest in the stock market.

- The occurrence of recessions, and the length of time the economy is in a recession, has decreased substantially (From 1900 to 1982 the economy was in a recession 30% of the time. From 1982 to 2000 that figure was reduced to 4% of the time. Less recession means fewer stock market declines which equals higher stock values and prices).

The rewards a profitable company returns to you for your investment in its stock are dividends and capital appreciation. Capital appreciation is achieved through the growth of the company's revenue base (achieved through increasing product/service lines, selling into new markets, mergers/acquisitions plus the automatic increase created by the CPI increase discussed in the previous section). Dividends are the immediate return an investor accepts in exchange for waiting for the capital appreciation to occur. Dividends are as important to the price of a stock as is the appreciation.

From 1976 through 1995 the S&P 500 Index had an Average Annual Return of 14.6% (a return reflective of the 51-year AAR). Reinvested dividends accounted for 59% of that return. A $10,000 investment into the Index on January 1, 1969 would have grown to $469,677 by December 31, 1999 if all dividends and capital gains were reinvested. If the dividends had been taken in cash, the $10,000 investment would have grown to only $159,597.

The price of a stock may be determined by many factors. Some of these factors are listed below:

- Hype of stocks from the media (news stories dispensing irrelevant or false information and more stories devoted to the stock market).

- The easing of margin requirements that allow more stock to be purchased on credit.

- Speculation into a stock or a segment of the market (fueled by both of the factors listed above plus the hype associated with the IPO market. Speculators are not concerned about the income of a stock or the potential for income. Their only concern is that they can sell at a price higher than the buy price and not get caught holding the stock when the price plummets).

- Investor expectation or anticipation on price (not value) movements of stocks based on information (valid and/or invalid) in advance of the various stock markets reacting to the information. This concept is largely responsible for short term price swings in both directions.

Recent history provides a perfect example of stock prices vs. stock values. The NASDAQ market received an incredible amount of attention from the news media, individual investors and brokerage firms who were able to profit by selling investment-related products or services as a result of the increased attention. The NASDAQ market, which celebrated its 30th anniversary early in 2001, closed at 2,192 at the end of 1998. At the end of 1999 this market was 4,069. On March 9, 2000 it closed at 5,046. Champagne bottles were uncorked in brokerage offices across America to celebrate the milestone and the tripling of the market that had taken place in less than two years. Video footage of stodgy brokers drinking the champagne became part of that evening's newscast. On December 31, 2000, the NASDAQ closed at 2,470, a 51% decline from the year's market high reached on March 10th and a 39.3% decline for the year 2000. As with any market bubble and burst, the price decline happened much faster than the market run-up.

What happened?

A combination of easy margin credit, media hype, speculation, greed and false anticipation that many internet companies would be able to report net income two to three quarters into the future. All the rules of stock valuations and Price-Earnings ratios were tossed aside by individual and institutional investors. Intelligent investors and unintelligent investors alike didn't want to miss out on the bandwagon. At the time the NASDAQ was trading at its lofty level of 5,000 plus, there were companies whose stock price was increasing weekly, if not daily. These companies had no net income and no chance of having net income at any point in the future. Instead of being able to calculate and report Price-Earnings ratios for these companies, analysts had to invest a new reporting category, Price-to-Revenue. Even some of the established companies with a track record of earnings such as AOL, Microsoft, Dell Computers, etc. were trading at prices that gave them P-Es so high that they would cause nosebleeds. During the summer of 2000 I checked the P-E of AOL. The number was 105.

There are two major lessons to be learned from this section.

Number One: The **VALUE** of a stock is tied directly to its earnings or the future earnings that a prudent investor with factual and unbiased information of the company's products, markets, finances, management team, etc. can expect to see. The **PRICE** is often determined by many factors...most of which have nothing to do with the value of the stock. Price does not always equal value.

Number Two: we have learned to control the money supply to the point where the high inflation of the 1970's will not occur again. However, we have not learned to control human behavior to the point we can protect investors from themselves and prevent them from rushing foolishly into market bubbles and bidding up prices. The same thing that happened to the NASDAQ market in 1999-2000 will happen again. I don't know when it will happen, but when it does happen, stay on the sideline. Let the uninformed, unenlightened and uneducated sit on the bubble. Don't let the media hype and the associated noise influence your decision to purchase stocks with a price tag way out of line with the value.

IV. Why Stocks are Your Best Investment

This section will be a recap of the information we've covered to date plus one major revelation. I will save the revelation for the end of this section, which will also be the shortest of the ten sections.

Stocks will be your best investment into the future because:

- Inflation rates will not repeat the lofty rates they reached in the 1970's and early 1980's. The absence of inflation will mean that the future return of the markets will be even higher than the historical averages.

- Increased contributions to defined savings plans, the increased prevalence of mutual funds, the consistent flow of dividends will maintain the value...and the price...of common stocks as investors are willing to accept higher P-E ratios.

- The yields on bonds will remain low because low inflation rates mean low bond interest rates. There will be limited possibility for capital appreciation for bond investors created by declining rates.

The best reason why stocks are your best investment has to do with the motivation of the people managing the companies you are investing in vs. the motivation of the people who issued the bonds you are buying or managing the bank whose interest-bearing instrument you are acquiring.

Individuals running publicly-traded corporations in this country have many responsibilities and duties. But above all their major charge is to enhance and increase the value of the stock of their company. They do this by finding ways to increase revenue, net income and cash flow. Be it new product introductions, mergers, acquisitions, cost reductions or new marketing strategies, the managers of corporations are attempting to increase the net income of their company so that the price of the stock increases by the P-E multiple. And if the people given this responsibility can't do it, they are shown the door and replaced by other individuals given the same duties. The managers of corporations are working for you. A large part of the compensation for upper management personnel are stock options and bonuses tied to the performance of the company. These options only have value if the stock price increases and the bonuses are rewarded only if the value and the price of the company increases.

Inversely, when you acquire a bond, the managers of that entity (be it a corporation or a government agency) are working against you. It is the purpose of the issuer to increase the value of the corporation (or credit-worthiness of the issuing government entity) to the point where they can issue bonds at a rate lower than the bonds you are holding and trip the 'call' provision so your bonds can be retired. The interest rate a bank pays you for your CD account or money market account is controlled by factors other than those that bank management can control. But the premise is the same. They only pay you the absolute minimum interest rate they can to get your money in the door. *In Part III of this story I will provide you more insight into the true workings of the banking industry and share some of my experiences in that business.*

Remember: ownership of stock represents ownership of a company. The managers of that company are working for you. Bonds and bank instruments are loans. The issuers of those instruments are working against you.

V. The Proper Way to
Buy and Own Stocks

One of my uncles had worked in the securities industry for a short time. Like many people before and after him, he obtained his license, tried to sell investments to other people and found that he didn't like the business when he couldn't make a steady living. When I was about ten years old, he took the time to teach me how to read the financial pages in the newspaper. I was able to identify certain stock and bond issues and study their prices, P-E ratios, dividends, and coupon rates.

When I was a teenager, having been influenced by things I'd seen on television, I remember thinking that an investment broker sat behind a desk with five different telephone lines and answered the constantly ringing phones with shouts of "Buy!" and "Sell!"

When I went to work for the gentleman who rescued me from the swimming pool hopper, one of my many job duties was to analyze various publicly-traded companies to see if there were any candidates for an acquisition or a leveraged buyout. In addition to the various real estate and banking work I did, part of my time was spent poring over the Annual Reports, 10-K statements, 10-Q statements and 13-D filings of various companies that had a per share asset base greater than their current per share market price.

When I first got my broker's license, people would ask my opinion on certain stocks. Since I was the proud owner of a Series 7 NASD license, I felt that some power had been vested in me from above that gave me the ability to talk about any stock issue...even though I had done absolutely no research on that company. The value of my opinion on the future of any stock issue was worth nothing. My opinion was much like the real return on a taxable bank savings account. It had negative value.

What's my point? The point is this--an individual investor...much less a person selling investments...does not have the time, resources, ability or access to the information that a professional mutual fund manager does. The evidence proving why we need to own stocks is overwhelming. The only question that remains is this: Should we pick and manage a portfolio of individual stocks or should we own stocks through the purchase of mutual funds?

The answer is easy: The most effective and efficient way to buy and own stocks is through mutual funds. There is one major reason why mutual funds are your ticket to stock ownership and three minor reasons.

Knowledge is the most valuable asset there is. Managers of mutual funds are in the business of gathering, analyzing, separating, discarding and confirming data. The data they are studying can be anything ranging from a meticulous review of a company's financial statements to a discussion among a company's customers, suppliers and/or competitors. You do not have the time or resources that a mutual fund manager has to perform the necessary research on a company's current and future prospects. A mutual fund manager or analyst can telephone any executive in any publicly-traded company in this country and have a conversation or meeting with that executive. If knowledge is the most valuable asset there is, the way to acquire that knowledge is through research. And mutual fund managers/analysts are better than anybody at performing investment analysis and financial research.

The result of a conversation or meeting with company management may result in a fund manager doing one of the most important things a professional money manager does for you...selling a stock whose time to sell has come. The investment history books are loaded with stories of companies who were once leaders in their industry or on the fast track to success but were derailed by poor management, overwhelming competition, drastic change in consumer taste or a combination of these factors. Individuals working at their job or running their business, families and homes and trying manage a portfolio of specific stock issues do not have access to the details and data that would lead them to sell the stock whose time to sell has come. Those same investment history books are full of stories of companies who once enjoyed a lofty position in their industry because of fictional accounting practices on the part of company insiders. (The SEC has recently been cracking down on this practice. There are people sitting in prison cells as I write this because they overstated their company's revenue/income and understated expenses all in the hopes of driving up their stock price.) The best people to detect accounting fraud are stock analysts employed by mutual fund companies.

In my files is a list of well-known companies with stock prices that experienced a dramatic decline over the twenty year period from 1972 to 1992. This list has been with me for a number of years, and I never knew until outlining this chapter what the best use for this list would be. You will notice that from 1992 until today some of these companies were acquired, merged or disappeared from the corporate landscape. Other companies were able to sustain themselves, retool their product line and markets and generate new revenue sources. They are viable and profitable businesses today but were in dire financial straits in 1992. Here are ten of the most recognizable companies from the list:

Company	Price Change 1972-1992
Avon Products	-59.5%
Black & Decker	-49.7%
Eastman Kodak	-38.6%*
Navistar International	-94.1%
Polaroid	-50.6%
Quaker State Corp.	-66.6%
Sears	-21.6%
Winnebago Industries	-68.4%
Xerox	-46.9%
Zenith Electronics	-89.2%

This decline would have probably happened even if Matt and I had been hired.

How many investors had these stock issues sitting in their safe deposit box in 1972 and rode the train down for the next twenty years? "Buy and hold" does not mean buy stocks with declining revenue and income streams and forget about them. Buy and hold means investing in stocks with solid, growing revenue streams and the ability to report income and pay dividends. If a stock you are invested in has a change in its fortunes, there is nobody who knows better when it's time to sell than a mutual fund manager who is doing his/her homework.

One of the best/worst stories I know about the dangers of owning individual stock concerns a gentleman I met in the mid 1990's. This man was a retired steelworker from Weirton, West Virginia. At the time of his retirement he was given shares of stock in National Steel, which later became part of the National Intergroup conglomerate. The number of shares was around 5,000 and at the time of his retirement National Steel was selling at a price in the low 70s.

The man rolled the stock over into his IRA and left it alone. National Intergroup took on too many things...too many companies, too many loans, etc. The stock price started a steady decline.

When I met the retired steelworker, NI stock was trading at $14.00 per share. His IRA value had decreased by over $280,000. When I asked him why he didn't reallocate his IRA shares after rolling them over, his sad reply to me was, "Nobody told me I could do that." The sadder thing about this story is that there are other people sitting on stock whose value and price has declined and they are relying on those stock issues to fund their retirement or the legacy they plan to leave to their children.

Did I scare you enough? Good. Now go own your stocks through a mutual fund. Here are the three more reasons why mutual funds are the best way to own stocks:

1. Mutual funds give you access to the international markets.

The reasons you need exposure to the international market are as strong as the evidence why you need to own stocks:

- 2/3rd of the world's stock market value is located outside of the United States.

- International investing provides more diversification and growth opportunities simultaneously.

- Developing countries provide growth opportunities through investments in infrastructure (Eighty-four percent of the world's population lives in developing countries. These countries possess 50% of the world's economy but only 15% of the world's stock market value). Many countries are infants compared to America in terms of their telecommunications, energy and financial service industries.

- Over the last ten years the S&P 500 Index had a AAR of 18% and the EAFE Index had a AAR of 7.5%. The EAFE AAR was substantially below its 30-year average of 14.22%. Students of Probability & Statistics will convince you that the next ten years will show above-average returns in the EAFE to return the LT averages to equilibrium.

2. **Mutual Fund Investing Provides Access to Other Valuable Services**
   - Through your investment in mutual funds you can take advantage of various pricing structures (Class A, B & C shares, Statements of Intention, Rights of Accumulation), reinvestment of fund distributions, automatic investing and withdrawal programs, and gifting and retitling of shares. Mutual funds also provide extreme liquidity.

3. **The Mutual Fund Industry is Highly Regulated**
   A detailed explanation follows.

The overt fraud that was conducted by the securities industry in the 1920's was largely responsible for the Crash of 1929. The behavior of brokers, bankers, and investors before the Crash was simultaneously stupid, humorous and bizarre. Without any rules and regulations to keep markets fair, promoters of stock issues were able to pull off numerous scams and entice people from all cross sections of life to invest money into worthless stock issues. Let me go off on another tangent here. If you're interested in reading a classic book, pick up John Kenneth Galbraith's *The Great Crash, 1929*. This book chronicles the multitude of events leading up to the October 1929 debacle and points the finger at everyone involved. The perpetrators included the brokers who saw easy pickings selling stocks with ever increasing prices (not values) to sophisticated and unsophisticated investors alike, to bankers who gave easy margin credit to stock speculators, to the media who touted the rising stock market as a way to provide every American with wealth and wipe out poverty. Galbraith also points the finger at the Federal Reserve who did nothing when they should have done something to slow the madness (i.e., increase the margin requirement which would have greatly decreased stock speculation) and then did the worst possible thing they could have done. Shortly after the Crash, the Federal Reserve strictly tightened the money supply. This sharp decrease in the money supply was the action that probably caused the Depression, not the market crash itself. Galbraith will be revered as one of the greatest economists of all generations and a gifted writer. I've read the book twice and found myself laughing at sections detailing the lengths upstanding members of society went to in order to take advantage of fellow members of society. It is important to note that there were similarities between the market frenzy of the late 1920's and the NASDAQ market happenings of the late 1990's. The same eternal optimism, the same suspension of the rules of P-E ratios and Price vs. Value and the same erroneous and non-objective information presented by the media was present. And you know what? At some point in the future, when the boom and bust of the NASDAQ market is forgotten, we will see another bubble when stock prices became totally unrelated to stock values and a bust when the prices fall back to earth.

With the organization of the Securities and Exchange Commission in 1933, the passage of the Investment Company Act of 1940 and the formation of the National Association of Securities Dealers in 1939 we now have an industry that is highly monitored and regulated. The SEC and NASD do a great job of bringing uniformity to the information that must be disclosed by mutual fund companies. The industry operates on a fairly level playing field when it comes to presenting returns, operating expenses and portfolio turnover rates to the public. The NASD is to be recognized for their aggressive work in dropping a penalty flag on false, deceptive and misleading advertising. The industry still has a long way to go to eliminate the overt fraud and deception that goes on in the industry. But this fraud is carried on by individuals and not the system. Until we can find a way to improve human behavior, investors will be subject to penny stock swindles, IPO issues that 'can't miss' and margin accounts that create havoc with credit ratings. By the way, the last sentence I've just written is another reason why you should invest in mutual funds and not individual stocks. The chance to be ripped off is much greater when you are dealing with individual stock issues.

In concluding this section, I want to leave you with this thought: Mutual fund managers and the stock analysts they work with are far and away the best in the business at performing research on businesses, countries, industries, people, etc. Research is the heart and soul of the investment business and I want to provide you with one of my favorite quotes:

"Research is a blind date with knowledge."

—Will Henry (American western novelist;1912-1991)

VI. The Cost to Buy Stocks vs. The Cost to Own Stocks

When I started my trek to learn the truth of investing money, one of the first areas I stumbled upon was the importance of asset management fees. Mutual fund managers and the brokers who sell their funds are charging you fees to select the securities in your portfolio and to perform the various administrative duties required by the industry. If you have an investment professional selecting a portfolio of stocks, that service also comes at a cost to you. If you are holding a portfolio of stocks that you selected or were given to you through inheritance or a profit-sharing plan and "non-managing" the portfolio, there is another cost you are paying. Economists refer to this cost as "opportunity cost." Most likely you are paying for not having professional asset management (and the research that comes with it) in the form of a reduced yield and changes in stock values that trail the overall stock market. Owning mutual funds or having your stocks managed by an asset manager also brings another expense. The amount of portfolio turnover brings about associated expenses known as transaction costs. The next section will deal with portfolio turnover and transaction costs. This section will deal only with the impact of high asset management fees on investment yields.

It was a moment of great illumination when I learned about high fees and low returns. My first foray into the arena of management fees began when I performed a study dealing with the impact of management fees on portfolio returns. I compared two fictional pension plan portfolios. Each portfolio began the study with $1,000,000, and each was going to earn a yield of 12% each year for 20 years. Portfolio A was going to pay 75 basis points per year in fees to have its assets managed (100 basis points equals 1%;75 basis points equals 3/4 of 1%) and Portfolio B was going to pay 1.5% per year. There would be no more additional contributions to either plan. The difference in management fees, 75 basis points, doesn't sound like much, does it?

Over any period of time Plan A will have more money than Plan B because of the lower fee. What is surprising is the difference. At the end of Year 10 the difference in portfolio values is $210,424. After Year 15 the difference has increased to $523,803. At the end of the study period, Year 20, the difference is $1,168,024. In terms of percentages the differences were 7.8%, 12% and 16.3%, respectively. The size of the difference in Year 20 really shocked me.

I turned my study results into an article. The article was written over a short period of time, and I was excited about both the relevance of the study and the quality of the work. The only problem was that I had no title for it. At the time I wrote the article, I was living in my parents' house. In the woods behind the house a large tree had split in half during a lightening storm. I took an axe into the woods to trim the tree and remove it from the path used by the deer that lived in the woods. I was cutting into the tree for about five minutes when the perfect title for my article popped into my brain. The title of the article, which told about the negative impact of pension plans paying high fees, became this:

Pension Plan Fees: A Pain in the Assets

I attached the title to the article and submitted it to *The Pittsburgh Business Times*. A few weeks after my submission I received a phone call telling me that the article would be published.

When I saw the article in print, I was disappointed and ticked off at the same time. The editors at the newspaper changed my clever headline to a plain headline that is not worth repeating here. They did some editing that was not necessary. To add insult to injury they misspelled my last name. When I called to complain...about the headline more than anything...I was told that they didn't want to offend any of their readers with my "risque" headline.

The article itself didn't create much of a stir. My phone didn't ring with investors wondering what fees they were paying to have their assets managed and what effect it was having on their overall return. I did receive two phone calls from mutual fund wholesalers who saw the article and telephoned me to compliment me on the thoroughness of my study. They didn't invite me to lunch, however.

What did happen after the article was published--but only as a coincidence--was that many other business publications began writing articles/studies on the importance of paying low fees for asset management. The Department of Labor, which has final responsibility for all the pension plans in this country, performed two studies detailing the negative impact high fees have on pension plan returns and posted the studies on their website (www.dol.gov). Just as a matter of coincidence, the publication of my article with the great title that didn't get printed was the beginning of the publication of a host of other articles dealing with asset management fees and portfolio yields. I'm happy now when I meet with a new client, and one of the early questions they ask me is the amount of commission and management expenses they will paying. Somewhere along the way, unlike investors from the previous generation, these people have learned that fees are important in determining the long-term performance of a portfolio.

What you need to know about asset management fees is this:

- A mutual fund manager or portfolio manager is entitled to charge you a fee each year.

- The average stock mutual fund manager charges 1.5% of assets each year for management of the assets.

- There is an established correlation between high management fees and low returns on mutual funds.

- Picking and holding various stock issues on your own will most likely cause an opportunity cost that will surface in the form of a reduced yield.

My article makes mention of ways the industry attempts to get you to pay more fees. These attempts usually come in the form of an investment salesperson attempting to 'wrap' a fee around the mutual fund fee you are paying. You are told this additional fee is so that the salesperson can better monitor your account and that the broker can 'rebalance' the account when needed. If you are asked to pay an additional fee (most mutual funds pay brokers a 25 basis point trailing commission each year), go find another broker. Your yield will be reduced by the higher fees. The number of times in your investment life that you need to reallocate assets is few (only when there is a major change in your lifestyle or you are about two years from turning growth-oriented assets into income-producing assets). You will make less, not more, money when paying higher fees. You will not receive more individual attention from a broker because of the higher fee you are paying. Many brokers generate the type of income they do because of the additional fees they charge. The only thing you will receive, as a result of the higher fees, are Christmas and birthday cards (I don't know about you but I am not a fan of those non-personal, non-sincere greeting cards sent by business associates and vendors).

The most important and serious item to leave you with about management fees is that if you are paying high fees to have your assets managed, you are not giving your assets the chance to take advantage of the Law of Compounded Growth. The more money going to an asset manager or investment broker means less money to earn dividends and capital gains on and compound. The best evidence of this statement can be found in the results of my study.

Regardless of what else I've learned or will learn about the investment business, this subject will most likely remain my favorite.

VII. Portfolio Turnover--
What You Make vs. What You Keep

This section is a sister to the previous section. Portfolio turnover refers to the selling and buying of securities in the mutual funds you own or in the portfolio of stocks you are holding. It is of importance because these transactions generate a cost to you in the form of capital gains taxes and the portfolio manager's actual costs of buying and selling. These costs are known as "transaction costs."

One of the commissioners of the SEC referred to high portfolio turnover as the "dirty little secret" among the mutual fund industry. On average, a stock mutual fund loses 2.5% of its return each year because of the capital gains taxes that the investor must pay. The issue became such a concern at the SEC that mutual fund prospectuses are now required to reveal their tax adjusted return next to their overall return when providing investment results. Some mutual funds now market themselves as being "tax efficient" and manage their affairs to keep their capital gain exposure as low as possible. I think this is just another in an seemingly endless stream of marketing ploys used by the industry. It wouldn't be prudent for a fund manager to sell a stock with a gain for tax purposes when the stock may still have capital appreciation in front of it.

Transaction costs provide another level of operating expenses to a mutual fund. The average stock mutual fund has a portfolio turnover rate in excess of 80%, and it is not uncommon for me to review a stock mutual fund with a turnover rate in excess of 100%. The average turnover rate means that 4 out of 5 stocks that are in a portfolio on January 1 are sold off by December 31. The funds with high turnover rates are often sold by investment brokers who preach the importance of investing for the long term and the "buy and hold" strategy and then sell mutual funds that do the exact opposite. The constant selling and buying of securities creates capital gains inside the fund but also increases the total cost of the fund. Go back to the discussion on management expenses. In my study on fees and portfolio returns, a 75 basis point difference in the management fee resulted in an ever increasing percentage difference in the value of the assets (by Year 20 the difference had grown to 16.3%). It is not uncommon for mutual funds with high turnover rates to add an additional 50 basis points to the total fee structure of a mutual fund. And that fee is on top of the average 1.5% management fee charged by the average stock mutual fund and any other fees a broker can get away with.

Stock mutual funds with a high portfolio turnover rate often suffer from poor research and inconsistent management. The successful mutual fund manager is one who possesses excellent research skills and consciously strives for low operating expenses and prudent portfolio turnover rates.

VIII. Asset Allocation--How to Avoid a 'Pain in the Assets'

If you notice, I plagiarized myself by adopting the title used for my article on asset management fees for this section. I'll have to check with an attorney to see if it is possible to plagiarize yourself.

I tell potential clients that what I do in theory is teach people about the mechanics of stocks and bonds, the impact of inflation on their investment dollars, and the importance of paying low management fees and making sure they have low portfolio turnover rates in their portfolio. What I do in reality for my clients is determine the best asset allocation for them and then provide them with the assets to fulfill that allocation. The concept of asset allocation is so vital that an often cited study performed by the SEI Corporation, a global pension plan management firm, revealed that 93% of a portfolio's return is tied to its asset allocation, and only 7% is correlated to individual stock selection and/or market timing. Allocation takes precedence over every other aspect of what I do for a client. It is so important that I pay the same attention to the asset allocation of a client with $1,000,000 as I do for a client with $1,000.

Everything we've discussed so far is part of asset allocation, and everything you've learned to this point is interrelated. The history and mechanics of the capital markets provide us with data on average annual yields and volatility of stocks and bonds, and the ever-increasing growth in the cost of goods and services teaches us the importance of investing against the loss of purchasing power.

There are two types of portfolios that apply to 99% of investors. The majority of the allocations are for investors who are investing for growth as opposed to income generation. The majority of this section will deal with growth-oriented investors.

The foundation for a growth portfolio is a combination of growth and income funds that are invested in American companies as well as international companies. The combination of dividend-paying stocks and stocks with growth potential will provide the most consistent growth with the lowest volatility. The next level consists of growth-oriented stocks that will provide higher volatility but that emphasize growth more than income and have a potential for higher returns as the companies in the portfolios began to generate or increase their dividend yields. Even my youngest investors, those with the longest time to let their assets grow, still have the majority of their money invested in growth & income instead of growth mutual funds.

Because of the reasons listed in Section VI about the importance of international exposure, a growth portfolio has to be invested overseas. However, we should recognize that any substantial USA-based corporation is deriving a growing percentage of its revenue from overseas operations and any foreign-based corporation is also generating revenue from selling its products and/or services to American consumers. This fact must be considered when structuring a portfolio.

Asset allocation is important, but it is also simple. There is not much I could write about the subject beyond what you just read, and many readers will already understand asset allocation. But what may be news to you is this: once invested, stay invested. Investors who think they can out perform the market by engaging in market timing or think a decline in market prices is the time to move out of the stock market invariably end up trailing the overall return of the market (and this does not take into consideration the increased transaction costs and possible capital gains taxes such moves entail). Two major studies provide great evidence why you need to stay invested in the proper range of asset allocations.

The first study was performed by Professor H. Nejat Seyhun of the University of Michigan. Professor Seyhun analyzed the 30-year performance of the Dow Jones Industrial Average from 1963 to 1993. The AAR of the Dow over that time period was 12%, and there were 7 years of negative returns. However, if an investor missed the 40 best trading days out of the 30 years, their return would be reduced to 7%. In monetary terms, if you had put $10,000 into the Dow Jones Index in 1963 and reinvested your dividends and capital gains, your investment would have been worth $233,000 by 1993. If you had missed those particular 40 trading days (a percentage of less than 1% of the 30 year period), your 1963 investment of $10,000 would be worth only $80,000 by 1993.

The second study was performed by Terrance Odean and Brad Barber, professors in the Graduate School of Management at the University of California, Davis. The Professors analyzed the portfolio habits of 78,000 U.S. households with investment accounts at a well-known discount brokerage firm. These are investors who haven't yet seen the light about investing in mutual funds. Their investments were being made in individual stock issues. The study was released in 1998 and supplied the investment community with great insight into the ill effects of reallocating or turning over a portfolio. The highlights of the study are listed below:

- From February 1991 to December 1996 the average U.S. household realized an AAR of 17.7%. The households with the most active turnover (20% of the sample) saw an AAR of only 10% due to the ill effects of reallocating their portfolio.

- Investors have a tendency to sell their rising stocks and keep or purchase stocks with lower appreciation potential. The stocks sold by the households to rebalance their portfolios during the study period outperformed the stocks acquired by 5 percentage points during the twelve month period after the change in the allocation. After 24 months the difference had increased to 8.6%.

- Women had lower turnover than men. The reward for the females' patience was a return that was 2.3% higher than the men (and that doesn't take into account capital gains taxes and transaction costs men would have paid).

The results of the study are clear. Once you have the proper asset allocation, don't just do something, sit there. Professor Odean summed up the results of this landmark study when he stated, **"Trading is hazardous to your wealth."**
Even though the investment business knows the importance of asset allocation and the adverse effects of excessive changes to a portfolio, it doesn't stop attempts to get you to change your allocation on a regular basis. Some investment salespeople try to justify their high fees by telling clients their account will be analyzed yearly and the necessary rebalancing will be done. The proof supplied in the section on asset management fees is overwhelming as to why you should not pay unnecessary fees on your assets and why you should turn your portfolio over as little as possible.

When it comes to the subject of reallocation of your assets, there are only a few times in your investment career when you need to change your allocation. All of these situations involve turning growth-oriented assets into income-producing assets (usually done in conjunction with retirement) or when you need to make a large cash outlay (such as a home purchase, a tuition payment, a business investment). I have done extensive research trying to find some magic formula that correlates the time period in which you should reallocate the growth assets needed to generate income or to satisfy the cash outlay. What I have found is that there are no statistically valid studies that inform us when we should convert growth assets into cash or income-producing assets. In this area I have relied on common sense, the age of the investor, the other assets of the investor, and the specific purpose of the reallocation. What I do for my clients is to remove any money they need in the next 18 to 24 months from the stock markets and put it into equity-income funds, bond accounts or money markets. I do have knowledge of individuals who needed to make tuition payments, home purchases, business investments, etc. within the 18-month to 24-month window and stayed at the dance a little too long. A downward fluctuation in the market caused a decrease in the value of their assets at a time when the investor could not afford the short term volatility of the market. Retirements were delayed, parents had to scramble among other sources for tuition money and home purchases had to be delayed due to the unwise risk taken by the investor. For the record, none of these people were clients of mine.

Allocations for investors in need of income from their assets are a different ball game. The purpose of saving money for most people is to accumulate enough funds so that they can turn the principal amount into an income stream. When doing so, the allocation switches from a majority of growth and growth & income funds into income-producing assets such as bond funds and equity-income funds. Growth & income funds are retained in a minority position so that the principal will still have appreciation potential (remember, your life-span after retiring may be in excess of 30 years). Inflation will wreck your assets and your legacy if you are not invested properly. In planning a retirement, I inform investors that they will probably need 80% of the income they earned pre-retirement. Assets converted from growth to income can be expected to yield an income stream of 6%. In planning at what asset level a client can retire, we contact the Social Security Administration to find the benefit level at ages 62 and 65. We then deduct the more attractive of these amounts (most often the age 62 benefit) from the required income and apply the 6% factor to the asset base of the client. For example: a person requiring a retirement income of $50,000 annually will be receiving $15,000 in Social Security benefits. The amount of assets this person has equals $400,000 (from a combination of IRAs, 401(k), non-qualified money). The 6% factor on $400,000 equals $24,000. The combined income stream of $39,000 would put this client $11,000 away from his/her targeted income stream. In this situation, the client would have to readjust their income expectations in retirement, extend their work-life one or two more years and add to their asset base or take a distribution from their assets higher than 6%. If the client chooses the last option, he/she may see an erosion to the asset base due to the higher than recommended cash outflow. He/she may also see a decrease in the amount of assets to be left to the heirs. This last situation has to be balanced out by a client's desire to leave the work-force and enjoy post-retirement years, family, hobbies, etc. Some of my clients have retired, rolled over their 401(k) assets into an IRA and started taking distributions even though their asset level wasn't high enough to support their desired income. Because of other circumstances (health, family, desire to travel) they retired and either readjusted their income level or obtained a part-time job to make up the difference. One of my clients, who was in his mid-50's, phoned me out of the blue one day and informed me that he had quit his job--two years before he was planning to do so. His assets weren't quite enough to allow him to retire. We applied a factor of 9% to his assets to generate the required income, and he works on occasion to supplement his income. He has a great allocation, appreciation in the growth & income segment and once he starts receiving SS benefits, we will decrease the amount of income he is drawing from his asset base.

The last and most important point to be made about growth or income asset allocations is this: there is a proper range for either type of allocation. As long as you are inside that range for your overall objective, you are doing the prudent thing. Too many investors waste too much time and energy trying to fine tune their allocation. They usually end up with a reduced yield, higher transaction costs and incur unnecessary capital gains taxes.

There are a few other related points to mention. When I am structuring an asset allocation for a client, regardless of the client's asset size, I never put the money into the various stock markets on any one day. I don't want to run the risk of any one or two markets suffering a temporary market decline on the day the investment is made. The money is placed into a money market account and then allocated into the growth/growth & income/equity-income funds over a 4- to 6-week period. One of my clients invested a large amount into a variety of growth and growth & income funds upon retiring from his company. We took a six-week period to move the money from cash into the funds. During the six week period the S&P 500 Index had a decline of 1.6%. Because the client was buying into the market on days when the market finished lower, he was able to achieve an increase in his asset base of 2.1% over the same six week period. Now, if the market had decreased 10% the day after we finished moving the money, I still would have done the prudent thing for the client. Because his assets are basically invested for the benefit of his children and grandchildren, his allocation is about 60% growth & income and 40% growth. A temporary decline in stock market pricing is irrelevant for this type of investor.

If you are in a position where you are accumulating or own the stock of one company, it is vital not to let your allocation get overweighted with that one stock. I performed research to determine the optimum amount of stock of one company that should be in a portfolio. I was unable to find any valid studies or statistically relevant research that gave me a confident answer. I tell my clients that they should have no more than 10% to 15% of any one stock in their portfolio. The final figure becomes a function of the history/future of the specific company, the relationship of the client to the company (if they were a founder or insider the discussion of how much stock they should retain takes on a whole different light), and the cost basis of the stock. If you ever need an example why you shouldn't be invested excessively in the stock of one company, remember the steelworker from West Virginia we discussed in Section V.

At the beginning of this section I shared with you the results of the SEI Corporation study on the importance of allocation (remember: 93% of a portfolio's return is due to the allocation while only 7% is tied to individual stock/bond selection and market timing). Section V made a strong case as to why you should own your stocks through mutual funds instead of trying to select individual issues. The reason why you shouldn't engage in market timing follows.

The long-term movement of the dividend-paying stock market is well documented. The return and volatility of the next five to ten years in the market can be approximated using the return and volatility of any five- to ten-year period. The direction of the market over any short term cannot be predicted with any level of confidence. The reason is that the long-term market is built on prudent behavior, knowledge of cash flow/net income of businesses, knowledge of yields on alternative investments, cost of living increases, etc. The short term movement of the market is largely subject to unsubstantiated or invalid investor expectations, extreme and unfounded exuberance, or maximum pessimism. Investors can buy or sell simply because they want to be the first one in on a stock issue before the price escalates or the first one off a down-bound train taking a stock price south. These decisions may be made on the basis of false information, hype, gossip, poorly researched news reports, etc. Short-term investors are more interested in outguessing the other short-term investors than studying the value of a company and its future prospects. The motivating factor to buy or sell can be partly attributed to the "herd mentality." Nobody wants to be excluded from the group that is buying the next "can't miss" stock, and nobody wants to be a member of the group that gets stuck holding a stock as its price disintegrates.

My theory is this: short-term market movements, up or down, are largely determined by human behavior and reaction to information that is often invalid and/or irrelevant. A market timer who is successful is going to have to be an expert in psychology and how diverse individuals of various ages, income levels and education levels will digest, process and react to information and how those decisions will impact the pricing (not the value) of stocks in various markets.

Market timing is a bet that places its money on how the human psyche will react to bits and pieces of information that is most often times irrelevant. The underlying value of companies is of little or no significance to a true market timer. Unless you're an expert on the actions and behavior of the diverse human race, don't waste your time and money trying to time markets. And next time you see a book on market timing in the bookstore or library, check to see where you're standing. It will probably be in the fiction section.

IX. Dealing With the Media
How to Separate News From Stuff Put in to Create More Space Between the Ads

I know exactly when the market will go up and when it will go down. And I will tell you...but not until the 11 o'clock news...and only if it's 'sweeps' week.

When there is a large drop in the Dow Jones during any one day's trading, one of the local television stations leads off its 5 o'clock news (which used to be the 6 o'clock news) with the financial reporter (who formerly was the traffic reporter) in the news room, necktie loose, shirt sleeves rolled up gripping the copy he just finished writing before the camera light was turned on him. As he speaks, he is trying to explain to us, the uninformed audience, exactly what happened to cause the market to take such a tumultuous dive. When the stock market slowly and methodically returns to the point it was the day before the decline and then passes it, the financial reporter is not brought back to give us a follow-up report.

During the big run-up of the NASDAQ market in 1999, the newspaper in my city ran daily stories of people whose stock portfolios were doubling and tripling quarterly, if not monthly, and what they were doing with their new found wealth. Stories of Initial Public Offerings and the instant paper millionaires they created littered the business section. An IPO Glossary started appearing once a week to teach us the jargon of selling shares of stock to the public. The Glossary had bold printing and was served to us in a Question & Answer format.

The same person supplying the answers was also probably supplying the questions. When the NASDAQ market imploded and the IPO market dried up, the IPO Glossary quietly disappeared as did the stories of easy wealth in the internet/biotech industry.

The Pittsburgh Business Times, the publishers and butchers of my article on asset management fees, published a front page (above the fold) article about a local company that was experiencing tremendous growth, was on an acquisition spree and was planning to do the obligatory IPO. Three weeks after the article appeared, the leasing company that had leased the office furniture to the featured business arrived at their offices and repossessed the furniture for nonpayment. That story never appeared on any page in any issue of *The Pittsburgh Business Times*

The reason these glimpses of life inside the media are important is that the media has become a factor in the short-term direction of the stock markets. Because of dramatic increases in the number of newspapers and magazines devoted to business and investing and the comparable increase in cable channels and television shows discussing the subject, there are too many pages and too much air time that must be filled. In their quest to do so, the media has advanced from reporting investment news stories to creating, advancing or burying them. The media has become a player in the list of variables that determine the price of stocks. Fortunately, the media has had little or no impact on determining the value of stocks. It is important that an investor realize the impact the media now has on stock prices and the proper way to deal with this newly created influence.

The media is not telling you about investment issues for your benefit. They are publishing and airing investment stories for their own benefit and for the benefit of their advertisers. The revenue source for the print media is not the money you pay for your subscription. Their income comes from the fees charged to advertisers who like your demographic group and have a product or service they wish to pitch you. Broadcast radio and television stations rely solely on the advertising revenue they generate, and cable stations derive their revenue from a mixture of advertising dollars and the cable-TV revenue paid to them directly by cable operators (and paid indirectly by you). What the media tells you about investment analysis takes a back seat to their quest to increase their audience base or improve the quality of their demographic so that they can charge higher advertising rates. The media will also not provide stories that may antagonize advertisers. Banks are big advertisers in newspapers and you rarely, if ever, see articles that supply data and insight into the numerous negative aspects of having your money in a bank account or a money market account.

The media does a good job of presenting news stories about business. Stories about mergers, acquisitions, bankruptcy filings, new products, new marketing strategies, employee reductions/additions, new plant openings or closings are presented objectively and are almost always well researched and well written. It's when the media presents stories about the stock markets that they lose their objectivity and the ability to do a proper job.

Too much media attention, especially on the television side, is spent trying to determine the movement of the stock markets over a short period of time. We know that the long-term trend of dividend-paying stocks is up. We also know that nobody, but nobody, knows the direction of any stock market over a period of time of less than one year. And anybody who tells you they do know is to be avoided. One of the most powerful and relevant sales tools I have is a list of quotes from three of the top investment minds of all time. Each of the quotes came in response to the question, "What Will the Market Do Next Year?" The quotes follow for your review.

> *"We don't have, never have had, and never will have an opinion about where the stock market, interest rates or business activity will be a year from now."*
> —*Warren Buffett*

> *"I have no feeling for the direction of the market over the near term, or the next three to twelve months--and that has always been my position."*
> —*Peter Lynch*

> *"Ignore fluctuations. Do not try to outguess the stock market. Buy a quality portfolio, and invest for the long term."*
> —*John Templeton*

In case you don't recognize the three authors of the quotes, Warren Buffett is the CEO and Chairman of the Board of Berkshire Hathaway Corporation. His ability to separate value from price is unmatched, and he is arguably the most successful stock picker of all time. As of this writing his net worth is in excess of $21 billion. Peter Lynch was the fund manager of what is now the largest mutual fund, Magellan, from 1977 to 1990. It was his research ability and ability to recognize trends among American consumers that lead him to invest in stocks that increased in both value and price and made Magellan the top ranking mutual fund in terms of assets. John Templeton was one of the first advocates of investing overseas and started the mutual fund company that bears his name. Mr. Templeton was an early pioneer into studying the economic, demographic, political and educational stability of various countries and determining which stocks of which countries would most likely lead to an increase in value and price.

These three men may be the best and the brightest in the investment business. If they admit to not knowing what the stock markets are going to do in the next twelve months, can we believe the talking head who is giving his opinion about the direction of the market or price of a specific stock after the commercial for the new and improved stock-picking service and right before the commercial for the other new and improved stock-picking service?

If you are an investment advisor or analyst, you are taught how to use the media to your best advantage. Investment salespeople are constantly trying to get their name into the paper or onto the airwaves to talk about investments. The importance of what is said is far less important than the fact that their name gets mentioned in an article or story dealing with investments. For some mysterious reason that I have never been able to understand, a large percentage of the population places trust and faith in people who appear on radio and TV shows and have their name show up in the newspaper on occasion. When you figure out the mystery, please let me know.

I will make one defense for the media. There is not enough information about the investment business for the number of stories or the amount of air time devoted to it. The basics of the business (the things we've discussed in Part Two) do not or will not change at any time in the future. The mechanics of the stock markets, valuations vs. pricing, the impact of inflation on your money, management fees, portfolio turnover rates, international investing, etc. just do not provide enough material to fill business sections of newspapers or air time of business TV/radio shows on a daily or even weekly basis. But the editors of newspapers and producers of business-related shows are under the gun each day to come up with investment stories. And because it becomes increasingly difficult to present different stories on the same subject, the quality of what is given to us is less than significant. That is the reason we get more stories that are irrelevant than stories that are relevant. My recommendation to the media is this: keep presenting stories on the few factors that are relevant. Write or air weekly stories about asset management fees and portfolio turnover rates. When short-term irrational behavior affects the markets, tell us that is what is happening. Don't bring in self-proclaimed experts to give their opinion about why the markets moved up or down. Use your creativity and resources to teach people how to invest money, how to react or, just as important, not react, when interest rates, investor behavior or market conditions change. The reinforcement and repetition of what really matters will make for better investors and help the audience/readers avoid losing value in their portfolios. This last one is a utopian wish. Many of the ads I see on business shows or in print are for investment products/service that definitely promise more than they deliver. Some of them are blatant scams designed to overtly separate you from your money and some are "quiet" schemes with a facade that appears to be professional but is still designed to separate you from your money. I doubt that these advertisers would continue to slot their ads in publications and on shows that are presenting stories on how to pinpoint an investment scam artist.

Another thing I wish the media would do is stop presenting stories about investors who make a tremendous amount of money in a short period of time and the changes in their lifestyle created by this sudden market wealth. When time becomes the final judge, it turns out that most of these individuals made their money through illicit trading activities, an overvalued and overly hyped IPO or some other means that enabled them to sell stock at a price much, much higher than the value. The truth about making money in the stock market is that it is not glamorous--it's boring. It is the sum of everything you've learned to this point--proper asset allocation, low management fees, low portfolio turnover rates and understanding the difference between a stock's price and its value. Inversely, the media should stop giving us stories about people with a dramatic decrease in their net worth caused by a declining market. A better use of space and time would be stories about the investment analysis issues that really matter. If we were given more educational and informative stories we would have less people losing their wealth due to market declines, inflated stock issues, and the dealings of unscrupulous brokers.

X. Putting it All Together

I'm a believer in the "Theory of the Declining Attention Span." This theory holds that the attention span of Americans has declined over the last decade. Some of the reasons given are an increase in working hours, an increase in leisure time alternatives, an increase in the number of cable channels, the MTV style of editing television shows and movies and, as reported in the previous section, an increase in advertisers' attempts to get your attention. The number of advertising outlets and the frequency of advertising grows each year. Nothing is sacred from the reach of those who want you to spend your money on their product or service. Witness the fact that advertising is now carried on the back of church bulletins.

My experience with a declining attention span is best found in baseball. When I was growing up I fully expected to play third base in the major leagues. I now find it uncomfortable and almost dreary to watch a baseball game in person or on television. The game moves too slow, my mind moves too fast, and I think about all the things I should be doing while watching the event.

In homage to the declining attention span, I will present this section as a summary of the previous nine sections. I will attempt to

'MTV' the relevant and pertinent facts, theories, history and real world workings of the investment business as presented to this point.

Here we go:

The ownership of stocks provides the highest potential return of any "passive" investment--that is, any investment that is not your own well-researched, well-capitalized and well-managed business. The last half century return of the S&P 500 Index (**14.32% Average Annual Return**) was significantly higher than that of Long Term Corporate Bonds (**6.49%**), Government Bonds (**6.37%**) and bank instruments (**5.12%**). Most important, the average inflation rate of **4.03%** meant that the real return of any non-stock investment would be reduced to **zero** (or less) once taxes were subtracted from the income stream.

Inflation will continue to stay low to moderate. The Federal Reserve Board and Congress will manage both the growth in the money supply and government spending so that we will not see the aberrational inflation rates that occurred between 1969 and 1981. The yields on bonds, Certificates of Deposit, etc. will continue to be just barely above the inflation rate. The **P/E Ratios** that investors are willing to accept for stock purchases may rise higher because of a combination of the public's understanding of volatility, the low inflation rate, low returns on fixed income investments and the continued investments into qualified savings plans, IRAs, etc.

The high return of the stock market comes with fluctuation which we call "volatility." Do not be afraid of volatility. The reward for understanding and being comfortable with volatility is the high rate of return that comes with the ownership of stocks. Much of the volatility of the stock market is created by irrational behavior on the part of investors. People tend to be overly optimistic and overly pessimistic. Don't let irrational behavior influence you. Don't forget what you have learned about **Price vs. Value.**

Buy and hold. Think about the work of Professors Odean and Seyhun. People who stayed invested in their proper asset allocation made substantially more money than those who moved in and out of the market. Even if you're a graduate and fan of Ohio State, you have to be impressed by Professor Seyhun's work done at the University of Michigan. By being out of the market for the **40 best trading days** in the 30-year period from 1963 to 1993, an Average Annual Return of **12%** would have been reduced to **7%**.

Your biggest risk as an investor is the risk of losing your purchasing power. This happens when you don't have the proper asset allocation. The cost of living doubles, on average, every **17** years. Think into the future. What are things going to cost? The only way you will be able to afford to live the lifestyle you're accustomed to is to be invested in the stock markets. Think about "tuition inflation" and "medical inflation." The increased costs in the future can only be overcome by proper allocation into the stock markets now.

Dividend-paying stocks should be the cornerstone of your portfolio. Remember: **over half** of the return of the S&P 500 Index has come as a result of the dividends paid by the companies that compose the Index. Invest internationally. It will increase your yield and reduce your volatility at the same time. As I write this, U.S. investors have only **7%** of their assets invested overseas. The EAFE Index had an AAR less than half of the S&P Index during the 1990's but had a similar return over the last 30 years. Where is the potential in the next ten years?

What is the best way to own stocks? Yes, that's right. Through mutual funds. Let the professional asset managers do the research and homework on which companies to buy and, just as important, which companies not to buy or which ones to sell. Did you see Oliver Stone's semi-classic movie *Wall Street?* Remember this line from Gordon Gekko: "Information is the most valuable asset I know of." And you cannot compete in obtaining and digesting information on businesses the way that a mutual fund analyst or manager can. Concentrate on your job, your family, your health and your hobbies. Let the professional asset managers select the stocks for you.

And when you invest in those mutual funds, what two things are you going to look for? Right again. Funds that charge you **low asset management fees** and funds that conduct their business with **low portfolio turnover rates**. Let's do a review of my article on asset management fees. Two portfolios. One paying **75** basis points, one paying **1.5%** for asset management services. A **12%** average return each year for **20** years. The end result? A difference of **16.3%** in value at the end of the period.

Turnover rates. Another layer of cost to you. Lower returns due to the increase in taxes and the historically lower returns from market timing. How important? It was a high ranking official of the SEC who called high turnover rates the "dirty little secret" of the investment industry. The average stock funds loses **2.5%** of its return each year due to the turnover of its portfolio. Think about the value of compounded growth on that 2.5% over a long period of time.

And lastly: When you are flipping through the cable channels and come upon a talking head in a Brooks Brothers suit telling you what to buy, what to sell, when to buy, when to sell...what should you do? The answer is simple. Turn off the television set and go do something productive. Take a walk, catch up on your reading, engage in a meaningful conversation with your family members or friends, do some volunteer work. And if you pick up the local newspaper and see headlines in the business section about the explosive growth of the stock of some new start-up or articles and columns discussing the direction of the stock market, what should you do? Easy. Turn the page. Go to the comics section. Read "Drabble," "Dilbert," "Beetle Bailey" and all the other insightful comics that provide a glimpse into the human condition while at the same time supplying a smile.

If you have the urge to read something about the investment business what you should do is reread this book. By taking my advice, you'll be more confident of your investment knowledge, less stressed, healthier, happier and more at peace.

And that's it. My MTV version of the Part Two review.

PART

THREE

This section is a collection of essays, some written independently of this book and some written specifically for this book. The essays are interrelated in that they will provide you with more insight into the investment business.

Before presenting the essays, I want to supply you with an update on the current status of Low-Income Housing Tax Credits. Almost everything you have read in this book about the subject of investing money I learned and wrote as a result of my inability to convince investors, accountants and other financial advisors that there was value investing in affordable housing.

Since Section 42 was put into the Tax Code in 1986, our country has developed about one million quality housing units for low- to moderate-income families, senior citizens and "working poor" individuals across America. The development of low-income housing is currently bringing 60,000 affordable units into the marketplace each year and the continued employment of 40,000 individuals in the construction and management of these units. About 35% of all multifamily housing starts each year are for low-income units. It always surprises investors to learn that many of the units are built in areas where the low-income definition (60% of area median income) is quite high. Housing costs in areas such as San Francisco, New York, Boston, etc. are so exorbitant that a blue collar working family has a next-to-impossible task of coming up with the money needed to make a down payment on a house and then qualifying to make the monthly principal and interest payments on a mortgage. The Tax Credit program benefits not only those families, but those cities as well, because more disposable income is spent among the businesses in the city instead of being exported to a lower cost town. My best example of low-income housing being anything but low-income is this: in Vail, Colorado an affordable housing development stipulates that a family of four can not make more than $115,000 per year in order to qualify for occupancy.

The Credits have become a big favorite of Corporate America. Because of the current tax law, corporations receive a greater benefit from investing in LIHTC than do individuals. The list of corporations with investments in low income housing reads like a 'Who's Who' of American business. About 2/3rds of the 30 companies that compose the Dow Jones Industrial Average have equity investments in Section 42 Tax Credits. Warren Buffett, through his company Berkshire Hathaway, has invested over $300 million in various funds that develop and manage affordable housing.

Individuals utilize Credits against their Federal tax liability, regardless of the source of the income that generated that liability. Probably the biggest use of Tax Credits for individuals is with those taxpayers who are in the Required Minimum Distribution phase of retirement. Upon reaching age 70$^{1}/_{2}$ taxpayers are required to remove money in regular planned withdrawals from all IRA accounts. The annual amount is based on their life expectancy and the market value of the combined IRA accounts at the end of the preceding year. By withdrawing money from their IRA accounts, a tax liability is incurred. Investors with Credits can lessen or eliminate the extra tax created by the distribution. I've sold Credits to individuals in their 70's and 80's who appreciated the fact they were able to reduce their tax liability while at the same time giving something back to society. As I was preparing the first draft of this book, one of my Tax Credit clients called me. He had just finished preparing his tax return and was happy to report that he was able to apply $7,000 of Credits against his tax liability. That's $7,000 he didn't have to send to the IRS.

When I first got involved in attempting to sell Section 42 Credits, the yield was 15% tax free. A taxpayer who invested $10,000 into a low-income housing partnership received the right to reduce their tax payments by $1,500 a year each year for a ten year period. The yield is a tax-free yield because the Credit is taken directly against your tax liability. It is a reduction of tax, not a deduction against income. For an investor in the 36% tax bracket, the 15% tax-free yield had a taxable equivalent of 23.45%. As the demand among corporations for the Credits increased, and as land and building costs increased, the yield on the Credits dropped. An individual investor purchasing Tax Credits now would receive a yield in the neighborhood of 10%. The taxable equivalent to an investor in the 36% bracket is still in excess of 15%. This yield is almost three times higher than the return on bank instruments and 2.5 times higher than the return on bonds. Once the tax benefits are figured in the yield is even higher. Yet, Section 42

Credits remain largely a mystery among investors, their accountants and their investment brokers.

Currently, about 5% of all U.S. households must spend over half their monthly income for rent and utilities. Because the demand for affordable housing continues to grow, Congress recently increased the amount of Credits available each year for investors. When the program was created, the amount of Credits available in each state was determined by multiplying the state's population by $1.25. The Credit factor was increased to $1.75 per capita in year 2002 and then indexed to the CPI factor in following years. This increase in the available Credits may result in an increased yield and more interest in the program among developers and investors.

One of the items that has always intrigued me about the program is the unique relationship between the private and public sectors and the fact that both political parties have been able to work together to provide a major benefit to the country's housing stock. The Democrats, long identified with social programs and consciousness, view the program as a way to provide quality, safe housing for low-income families. Republicans see the program as a way to lessen the role of government in housing, give more power to the private housing industry, and as a way for both corporate and individual taxpayers to decrease their tax liability. Both parties probably appreciate the improvement in the aesthetics of low-income housing, a major improvement over the generic red brick, lifeless box buildings the public sector was famous for building.

One of the ancillary benefits that Tax Credit housing has provided is a positive synergy for some of the tenants. A percentage of the units are built in mixed-use developments. Affordable units are interspersed with market rent units. People who have been living in public housing boxes are moving into units built by the private sector and moving next to individuals and families who have developed the work and life-style habits of people who have not been in public housing for multiple generations. This changed environment may have a positive impact on the future of the affordable housing tenants, their families and the generations to come.

When I first thought about writing this book, I knew I would need to write about Section 42 Tax Credits. I thought I would write a chapter about the mechanics of affordable housing, about the people who benefit from it, and about why I became so passionate about a part of the IRS regulations. I thought about finishing the chapter by writing these words: *If you are reading this book while sitting in a comfortable, solid house with a furnace that works when you turn it on, windows that don't allow winter into your living room, appliances that do what they're supposed to do, and that house is in a safe and established neighborhood you should be nothing but thankful. And when you think of the people who reside in low-income housing, don't think of them as people who don't work as hard as you, people who aren't as educated as you or people who don't deserve a solid and safe place to live. Think of them as people whose situation in life is dictated solely by time, place and circumstance.*

That's what I thought about writing and I just did.

The first essay, *The Usual Suspects*, provides insight into the lengths that sellers of investment products will go to make you a client. *How the Real Estate Business Really Works* is my personal love letter to my experiences in and around the real estate development business. The essay serves a purpose for this book and that purpose can be diagnosed from the subtitle, *Why Banks are the Worst Place for Your Money*. *Thinking About Money* details the field of behavioral economics. This growing field, also known as investor psychology, has been used by the business for years as a way to identify customer characteristics that could result in sales. Investors are now starting to use the techniques of behavioral economics to learn why they do the things they do with their money and as a way to remove the human psyche from the process of investing money, which should be an objective, non-emotional activity. Part Three concludes with a collection of short marketing newsletters that were written during calendar year 1999 and sent to CPAs and pension plan sponsors in the Pittsburgh area.

The Usual Suspects

Snow covered the golf course at the prestigious South Hills Country Club. There had been a late March snowstorm in Pittsburgh, but nobody had golf on their mind this evening. They had come to the SHCC, dressed appropriately for the location, because they had been invited to an investment seminar. They came in response to the embossed invitations that had been sent to their homes. Their names were put on a mailing list because they matched a certain income and age demographic or because their name had been submitted to the host during a previous seminar.

The quality and variety of the food on the buffet table was the equivalent of the offerings for any wedding or anniversary celebration held at this club. A chef, sporting his chef's hat, stood at the end of the table slicing lean roast beef. Wine was available for those who wished to imbibe.

After moving through the buffet line, the guests found a spot at one of the round tables set up for the occasion. Quiet and polite conversation was mixed in with the sounds of eating. Nobody laughed too loud or offered too much in the way of conversation. Most of these people were strangers to each other. For the vast majority of them, it was the first time in their life they had been in this country club even though most lived in the immediate area. Servers appeared without being summoned to refill coffee cups and water glasses.

As the meal neared its conclusion, a short, middle-aged man walked to the front of the room. He let the room know that the featured speaker would be beginning his presentation in fifteen minutes. He tried to build some anticipation in the room, but his efforts failed. He asked the guests to make their way to the dessert table one last time and to prepare themselves for the arrival of the their host. Before he departed, he let the audience know that the host, in addition to being an investment advisor, was also a committed Christian who was deeply involved in his church, was a committed husband and found time to coach his son's soccer team. Any audience member who was contemplating what to do with an IRA Rollover or investment portfolio could do no better than to let the host manage their money. Before he departed, the short man let the audience know that the host was the investment advisor of choice for Father Truman at the local church.

The host appeared from nowhere. He had not been in the room among the dinner guests. The way he appeared made you think he was in a side room working on a difficult investment problem for one of his clients or diagraming a new play for the soccer team. He strode to the front of the room and turned to greet the audience by extending his arms. He wore a black turtleneck sweater and a black blazer. The gold cross he wore outside of his sweater gave the impression that he had a connection to religious matters that the audience didn't.

He began by reiterating his devotion to his wife and child and his missionary work. He then produced a post card and informed the audience that it was sent to him by a couple who had entrusted their life savings to him. Because of his insight into the investment markets and his unmatched investment ability, the couple was able to retire early, afford a mobile home and spend their time touring the country. This story was followed with more stories about clients who were in financial turmoil until they came to a similar seminar. After feasting on the dinner, they turned over their savings or IRA accounts to him, and they now are also touring the country in a mobile home or doing the special things they wanted to do in retirement. If any member of the audience requested it, the speaker would give them Father Truman's number. If you called and he wasn't busy in confession or organizing a bingo, Father Truman would also tell you how adept the speaker was at managing money.

The speaker's marketing director, who happened to be his brother, approached the front of the room with 10 crisp $20.00 bills. The speaker began asking questions of the audience. The questions were simple, somewhat inane and mostly rhetorical. The questions were along the line of, "What would you rather do--send money to the IRS or use that money to take a trip to Europe?" and "What would you rather do--send money to the IRS or give your children money for the down payment on a house?" If you answered one of the questions, the marketing director/brother gave you a $20.00 bill. The speaker told the audience he passed out the money because he knew he would keep the attention of his audience by doing so. Maybe it was fatigue or maybe it was the brother's limited range but the money went only to the people sitting at the tables in the front of the room. Somebody in the back of the room remarked that if they had known money would be passed out they would have sat closer to the front of the room rather than taking a position close to the dessert table.

The investment advisor spoke for forty minutes. In that time he never mentioned anything about asset allocation, asset management fees, portfolio turnover rates, investment research or the other relevant components of investment analysis. He spoke of satisfied clients and the great wealth he created for others and his own feelings of self-worth when he thought about all the good he was doing for the world...or at least Pittsburgh. He also made repeated mention of his professional designations by referring to them as "the alphabet after my name."

Before the advisor took questions, he informed the audience that the first five people in attendance who signed up for a free one hour consultation in his office would receive a gift certificate redeemable at a fine dining establishment located in downtown. Interested parties were instructed to give their name and phone number to the marketing director/brother for he was the keeper of his brother's "book."

The first question came from a burly man at the back of the

audience. He asked if the advisor would be available to him via telephone if he needed to speak to him. When the advisor assured the man he would be, the burly man wanted to know if he called at 5:00 P.M. would the advisor take his call. When the advisor promised he would do so, the burly man asked if a phone call would be taken at 6:00. The advisor informed the man he was almost always in his office at 6:00. The burly man pressed on. How about 7:00? Probably not, according to the advisor. After all, he did need some time with his family and to perform church work.

Another woman wanted to know the name of the restaurant she would be eating at if she took up the offer for the free one hour consultation and the gift certificate. Unfortunately, that information could not be divulged to the audience. They would have to trust the advisor and his marketing director/brother that they would be sending them only to a highly regarded dining establishment in the city. A follow-up question came from a gentleman who wanted to know if the advisor validated parking. The answer to that questions was "yes."

The speaker had questionnaires for the audience to fill out. In addition to questions about age, income, net worth, size of retirement accounts, and the best time to be contacted, there was a section where you were asked to supply the names and phone numbers of five of your friends or co-workers who would be interested in attending a similar seminar.

The audience was informed that the seminar was over, and the advisor looked forward to working with each and every person who was in the room. The crowd started moving to the back of the room toward the exits. A man who had been silent during the question and answer session made his way to the front. He had a financial problem that was too complex to be shared with everybody else. He had a net worth so huge that he deserved some individual time with the advisor in the front of the room. As he made his way through and around the departing audience walking in the opposite direction, he made one think of Walter Payton dodging would-be tacklers to get to his destination.

The temperature had dropped since the seminar began. March was not supposed to be this cold. The people who had been in attendance at the meeting got into their cars and drove single file down the long driveway and away from the elegance and opulence of the South Hills Country Club. As they drove to their modest homes in the middle-class neighborhoods that surround the club, the thing they probably thought about most was the quality and amount of the food.

The scene you just read about is repeated every night in every city across America. It takes place in hotel meeting rooms, in the back of church social halls and even in country clubs. It is one of the major tools used by investment advisors to attract new clients. This seminar featured the two items advisors rely on most--free food and stories of clients who are happy, healthy and financially well off, all because of what that broker did.

The seminars usually take place in a hotel meeting room, a hotel the quality of a Holiday Inn. Nice enough but not too nice. Above the level of a Ramada Inn but below the level of a Hyatt or Radisson. This country club seminar was the exception, not the rule, for one of the Usual Suspects. During the middle of the week in March, there probably was a nice discount for the room and food.

What is a Usual Suspect? In investment parlance, it is a salesperson who realizes that gaining the trust of potential clients, by whatever means possible, is the key to closing the sale. Usual Suspects frequently host hotel seminars with stuffed chicken and sauteed mushrooms in the hopes that the audience members will talk to no other investment professional and will not attempt to learn independently anything about the investment business beyond what was told to them at the seminar. The Usual Suspects hope that the fact they give you food and drink will make you feel obligated to them and not wish to talk to any other investment professional.

Usual Suspects rarely tell you anything relevant or important about proper investment analysis. They will never tell you about the negative impact high asset management fees have on your portfolio yield. The reason deals with the way Usual Suspects sustain themselves. It is the high fees they charge to clients, maybe previous seminar attendees, that pay for the rental of hotel meeting rooms and off-season country club meeting rooms and food that future seminar attendees will consume.

The seminar at the South Hills Country Club had heavy doses of two items that the Usual Suspects have learned make them effective marketers: religion and family. It was no coincidence that the speaker dressed the way he did or made repeated references to his clients in the clergy or his involvement with the church. The Suspects have found that this gives them a level of trust among the public, and they play on it as much as possible. There are many sellers of investment products who routinely do seminars at church halls, advertise in church bulletins and join multiple churches as a way to generate sales leads.

An investment salesperson who has high family values must also be trustworthy, honest, and more interested in your best interests than his or hers. At least this is what the Usual Suspects want you to believe. Because investment brokers have discovered they can attract clients when they provide audiences with examples of their family values, they will continue to lead with details of coaching soccer teams and being supportive spouses and related "feel good" stories as a way to get your money. However, much the same way the advertising industry paints an image of a product that is different from what you buy, Usual Suspects may have gone too far in their quest to use the 'family values' pitch. The investment advisor who spoke repeatedly about his wife and child at the South Hills Country Club on that cold March evening actually had been divorced from three different women before finding marital bliss with Wife No. 4.

The Usual Suspects have also learned to use the media to their advantage. In my city, the weekend radio airwaves are crowded with investment shows where a broker or brokers receive phone calls from listeners. The one or two hours devoted to the typical show is acquired by the investment brokers under a contract with the station. Telephone calls are fielded on various investment topics, and the hosts provide an answer along with a constant repeating of their office telephone number. The cost of the air time can be expensive, and the brokers usually are required to occupy the air time for a minimum of one year. Where do brokers come up with the money to buy the air time? Of course. From the high management fees charged to their client base.

There are two types of callers to these shows. The majority of the calls come from people who appear to have no knowledge of investment or finance matters. They are probably hard working, blue collar people who come into money through the accumulation of profit-sharing assets, inheritance or divorce. Their lack of financial sophistication is perfect for the format of the show because the investment host or hosts are doing their best to chase unsophisticated dollars. The second, and less frequent, type of caller is the person who is a regular reader of *Forbes* and *Smart Money* and similar magazines and may be a frequent watcher of the financial shows on CNN or CNBC. They have a knowledge of the basics of investment analysis. But the knowledge is limited and limited knowledge of a subject may be more dangerous than no knowledge at all. These callers rattle off their stock or mutual fund holdings to the host. They supply the information in such a way that the listener can tell it is being given out of a sense of boasting or flaunting on the part of the caller. These calls are short in nature and usually end with the host inviting the caller to come to the office for a review of their portfolio at which time the caller announces he or she is happy with their portfolio and not looking for a change. Usually at this time in the show, the hosts must take a break and do their best to end the phone call. *I listen to these shows on a regular basis. My reasoning for listening is that I want to hear how much bad information is given out or how much relevant information is* ***not*** *given to the callers.*

Investment people are also continually on the prowl for free publicity. They routinely supply the finance reporters of local newspapers and TV shows with historical facts and figures about the stock markets, ideas and tips for retirement planning and other related information in hopes of having their name mentioned in print or broadcast over the air. Usual Suspects also keep their fingers crossed hoping to get a call from a reporter working on an investment story. Quotes from experts are standard fare in such stories. Because reporters cannot find any experts, they usually contact one of the Usual Suspects for a quote. One of the Usual Suspects I know keeps a running total of articles his name and quotes appear in and provides this to potential clients. This has proven to be a better sales piece than any article or essay this Suspect can write on any component of investment analysis, portfolio structuring or asset allocation.

Image is also a key item for the Suspects. Style is definitely more important than substance. I was once regaled in great detail by one of the Suspects about the time and effort he spent in choosing his office furniture, carpeting, art work hanging on the wall, and even the saucers and cups in which he serves coffee to his visitors. This particular Suspect once produced an audiocassette that supplied his theories on investing. The final product was delayed for a month because the photographs taken for the cassette cover didn't do a good job of hiding this Suspect's hair weave, and a suitable photograph had to be air touched before being put on the cover.

Part of the image factor for the Suspects is their automobile. One firm that specialized in the sale of "penny stocks" required their brokers to wear only black, blue or gray suits (pinstripes were acceptable) and the brokers were allowed to drive automobiles from a short list of expensive German automobiles. The parking lot of this company looked like something from the movie *Boiler Room*. One of the brokers who worked at this firm left town in a hurry when the Securities and Exchange Commission came to town to shut down their fraudulent operations. He ended up working construction in New Jersey under a false identity and came back to Pittsburgh only after agreeing to testify against his firm and the office managers and getting amnesty from the IRS.

There is a story I know about one of the Suspects who leased a Porsche while selling securities for one of the largest firms in the city. I'm sure he made a nice impression arriving at the home of potential clients in that car, which was its exact intended purpose. When his lease payments became too high for him, he hired somebody to steal his car and have it end up in the river. The story took an interesting turn when the car thief decided he wanted to have use of the car for a few days before sinking it. The Suspect reported the car stolen thinking it was in the bottom of the Monongahela River, when in fact it was being used by a different type of suspect to impress a different type of client. The thief got busted in the car. Imagine the Suspect's surprise when the police showed up at his office to inform him that his stolen car has been found, and the car thief couldn't spill out the true story fast enough. The firm this broker worked for is infamous for bizarre occurrences. During a Christmas party a few years ago one of the brokers was kidnaped by Santa Claus (no kidding) because the person under the Santa costume felt that it was the broker's fault his portfolio had suffered a tremendous decline in value. I don't know the facts of the case, but knowing brokers the way I do, I probably would take the side of Santa over the broker. Santa took the broker to a house in a neighboring county and kept him tied up for a few hours before releasing him. Another story that came out of this firm while I was writing this essay concerned one of their brokers who forged the signatures of his mother-in-law and father-in-law on documents that gave him access to their accounts and "discretionary authority." This forged document allowed the broker to generate commissions for himself while depleting the value of the portfolio. During the hearing that ended with the broker surrendering his license, he supposedly told his in-laws after they discovered the activity that they shouldn't take any action against him because... *"it would upset their daughter."* The daughter divorced her husband shortly after his deeds became known to her.

Unlike the Suspects with the problems centering around car lease payments that were too high and commissions that were too low or forging documents, most of the Usual Suspects do not do anything illegal. They do many things that are to their benefit and to the detriment of the client, but these things are not considered illegal. Making sure that the Usual Suspects' behavior does not cross the line of illegal activity is the Broker/Dealer. This is the entity that actually employs all brokers. The stated purpose of the B/D network is to make sure that individuals selling investment products are adhering to the rules and regulations of the National Association of Securities Dealers and the Securities and Exchange Commission while providing the required professional Continuing Education and sales ideas. In reality, what a Broker/Dealer does is provide a place for a broker to place their license while siphoning off a percentage of the sales commissions generated by the broker. The percentage of a broker's revenue that is kept by Broker/Dealers ranges from 60% to 10%. The lower payouts are offered by firms who provide a desk and a telephone for use of the broker along with business cards. B/Ds who offer the higher payouts basically require the broker to set up their own office and pay all their own expenses. Broker/Dealers are business entities and, like any for-profit entity, survive by the profit they generate. The only source of revenue they have is the commissions and management fees generated and charged by the independent contractor brokers whose licenses they are holding. I have been affiliated with five B/Ds and cannot think of anything positive to say about any of them or the Class B suburban office buildings they occupied.

Because they don't have to pay salary or benefits, some B/Ds will contract with anybody who has a reasonable expectation of passing the licensing examination. The thought process is that if a person can pass the test they may be able to induce their family and friends to turn over their investment accounts, and the B/D will be able to increase their income stream. If the person can attract clients beyond their family and friends, there will be more revenue to the firm. If not, the cost to the B/D is minimal as there was virtually no investment on their part in training the broker, and they may generate trailing commissions based on the sales the new recruit did close. I know of a B/D who charges anybody who walks in the door a $500.00 fee to take classes that will enable them to sit for the license examination. This fee probably constitutes a high percentage of the total revenue to the firm.

Other types of B/Ds put some thought and effort into whom they hire. Applicants at these firms are subject to a more intense interview process, aptitude and personality questionnaires, and often times are asked to submit a list of people they could contact to discuss invest-ment planning if they were hired. I was interviewed by two of these companies, both well-known names in the field of investment/insur-ance planning. On both occasions I was given a test to determine whether or not I had the personality and people skills that would enable me to become a successful broker. Both times I failed the test and had my application terminated. The human resources person for one of the companies, Mutual of New York (MONY), revealed to me that I had received one of the lowest scores ever given in their Pitts-burgh office. *(Maybe I should find a new line of work)*.

Broker/Dealers are forever trying to increase the sales output of their brokers. I was once affiliated with a Broker/Dealer that held monthly sales meetings at a local Holiday Inn. The meeting started with the sales manager discussing new sales ideas and ways to get more money from existing clients. Then, new business was discussed. This usually consisted of a change in the relationship between the firm and the brokers. This firm was constantly changing sales requirements, payout levels and mandatory insurance coverage. We would next be subjected to sales pitches from two or three wholesalers employed by investment companies (who do you think paid for the meeting room and the doughnuts and coffee?). Each wholesaler got twenty minutes to explain to the captive audience why we should be selling their mutual fund or limited partnership. The wholesalers were basically the same person. They looked different, they had different names and could have been of either sex. But they were all the same person. They talked the same way, told the same jokes and bragged about their employers in the same manner. The reasons why we should sell their fund or partnership contained more hype than substance, more fiction than fact. I attended about six months' worth of these meetings and then stopped going. I wasn't learning anything, and I got to the point where I couldn't bear to be in a roomful of brokers. It was a combination of the way they talked about their clients, their worthless opinions on the short-term movement of the stock market, and the less than stylish way they dressed. All of this gave me an uncomfortable feeling, similar to wearing a wool suit that itches and not being allowed to scratch.

Broker/Dealers will tell you they are a necessary player in the investment world, and one of their biggest responsibilities is to make sure that brokers receive the required thirty credits of Continuing Education each year. I'm on both sides of this fence. I give CPA's Continuing Education as well as being subject to receiving annual CE. The quality and level of the class work is lightweight;there are numerous easy avenues to getting the credit (such as attending seminars sponsored by wholesalers, taking internet classes or listening in on telephone conference calls). I remember sitting in front of a computer last New Year's Eve taking two internet classes so I could satisfy my CE requirements before year's end. There isn't one thing I can think of that I learned from complying with CE that has made me a better investment professional or that has helped me to deal with my clients better. Accountants are able to obtain their CE by watching videos approved by their firms, attending seminars similar to the ones I attend, or taking classes at local colleges. When I teach CPA's I remind myself of teachers I had in high school. When the accountants try to catch up on their reading or start to daydream, I stop my lecture and ask them to repeat what I've just said or ask them a question on the material.

The pursuit of continuing education in the investment business is too easy, and the level of the material doesn't benefit the participants or their clients. The ease of CE benefits the B/D's because they are able to maintain their revenue stream without expending too much effort or expense in keeping their employees in good standing with the NASD. The whole concept of CE in my business reminds me of something the great athlete Kirk Gibson said a number of years ago. Gibson was an All-American wide receiver at Michigan State and played in the major leagues with the Detroit Tigers, the Los Angeles Dodgers and the Pittsburgh Pirates. When somebody asked him what he majored in at Michigan State, his reply was "Staying eligible." Kirk's quote holds true for most of my fellow brokers when it comes to CE.

In my city there are about 15 to 20 Usual Suspects. This is the number of investment people who have been able to take advantage of Holiday Inn seminars, radio call-in shows, free publicity in the newspaper and on TV, and their church affiliations to obtain clients. Before I learned how the investment business really worked I had achieved a certain level of interest and expertise in Low-Income Housing Tax Credits. I attempted to approach various Suspects and work with them to educate their clients about Section 42 Tax Credits and the huge demand for affordable housing in America. Not one of the Suspects took the time to learn about the history, mechanics or value of Tax Credits. Not one of the Suspects took the time to learn how their clients could lower their annual tax expense and invest in a much needed part of the infrastructure of America. Nobody wanted to work with me. One of the Suspects, who had an investment call-in show on the local Christian radio station (he was using two of the tools the Suspects like to use-- religion and radio) told me he thought of his audience as his "ministry" and would never discuss a subject such as low-income housing with them. This is not my idea of a good Christian.

It was the job of the Usual Suspects to learn about Section 42

Credits and, for the most part, they did not do their job. Instead of learning about an investment that would provide value and benefit to clients, they spent their time trying to write the perfect "cold calling" script, or trying to determine the best menu to offer at their hotel seminars, or working on the china pattern for their offices. *(The newest hook for the Suspects--teaching non-credited classes at the local Community College. It's a way to get in front of potential clients. The material presented in class is secondary to the "free" financial plan each student has written for them.)*

Any one of the Usual Suspects could have knocked me out of the investment business. Any one could have prevented me from gaining a foothold in the business and learning about asset management fees, portfolio turnover rates, asset allocation and everything else you've read in this book. Any one of them, by just doing what they were supposed to do, could have prevented me from writing a book titled **How the Investment Business Really Works** and by writing a chapter titled *The Usual Suspects*.

How the Real Estate Business Really Works

Subtitled

Why Banks Are the Worst Place for Your Money

I have a confession to make. Early in this story I told you about my experiences working at the swimming pool construction company. I talked about how I liked putting my work boots on in the morning and how I liked the tight feeling of my work clothes as I started to put some muscle on my body. I relayed that I enjoyed driving around in construction vehicles and the ongoing dialogue about life, girls and our futures in the construction industry that was seemingly nonstop.

This is my confession: While I sincerely enjoyed my time on the construction crew, and I have incredibly strong memories of the things listed above, I was not terribly talented at the actual work. I did not have the gift for working with power tools, I was never able to master the art of finishing concrete and, as a Bobcat or backhoe driver, I was a danger to the people and property around me. But I liked construction, and I liked the concept of developing buildings for people and houses for families. When I developed my talents in economics, I knew I could work for real estate developers from the financial and marketing side. I could determine the value of a building. I could determine the income stream of a real estate investment and determine the maximum amount of development costs that could be spent in order to make the project successful. I could study a raw piece of property and determine the type of building that would make the highest and best use of the land. I could study a vacant and neglected building and determine which type of renovation would best fit the structure. I could use my knowledge of finance to locate the optimum source of financing for each project. I could work with the architects, engineers, construction companies and supply houses. I had such passion for building that each of these professionals would be as excited to work with me as I was to work with them. I was so enamored with the concept of overseeing the building process that at one point I equated the term "real estate developer" with the term "major league baseball player." That's the level of respect I once had for real estate developers.

Chapter 5 was introduced with a quote by the great novelist James Baldwin. *The price one pays for pursuing any profession, or calling, is an intimate knowledge of its dark side.* I used that quote to share with you my revelation that the investment business was much murkier from the inside than it was when I had the view of an outsider. I've seen the dark side of the investment business, but I've also seen the pitch black side of the real estate business.

I've been involved with every single aspect of the real estate business. The job I got after I left the swimming pool hopper gave me the opportunity to do acquisition, leasing, sales, lending, borrowing and everything else that is part of the business. I had the opportunity to work with numerous real estate developers and investors, banks, and real estate/mortgage brokers. The lessons I learned became invaluable. The insight I was afforded was invaluable. One of the most relevant things I learned was that the 'real estate' business should be called the 'fake estate' business. Except for the actual bricks and sticks that make up the physical properties, there is not much real about the industry. Much like strip clubs, the weight-loss industry, and the industry surrounding body building and exercise, it is a business built on illusion.

My expectations of working closely with architects and contractors were never met. Most of my experiences were in the financial and valuation side of the business. Because I worked for a successful real estate developer who started his own bank, I got to work on both sides of the fence and obtain insight that few people are lucky enough to gain access to.

Every party in this business is attempting to inflate their position in their dealings with the other parties in the industry. They do this by making vague and misleading statements and withholding vital information.

Contractors attempt to take advantage of developers, developers attempt to take advantage of tenants and lenders, tenants attempt to take advantage of developers (at the same time the developers attempt to take advantage of them), buyers attempt to take advantage of sellers (at the same time sellers attempt to take advantage of them), and brokers attempt to take advantage of buyers, sellers, and lenders. The only entity that takes advantage of no one but gets taken advantage of by everyone is the lenders.

One of the stark realizations I had to learn about the real estate business is that most of the industry depends on developers and investors taking advantage of bankers and other lenders. I formerly thought that real estate people made money by building their buildings, signing leases with tenants, collecting rents, paying their bills, taxes and mortgage payments and then putting the remainder into their pockets. Their big payday, I thought, came when they sold a property that had appreciated in value to another investor who started the process over. But that's not the way a developer or investor makes money. Developers and investors make their real cash when they borrow money. The more money that can be borrowed, the more cash that goes into the pocket of the real estate developer/investor. And because that money is in the form of a loan, it flows into those pockets without any tax liability.

At the center of the fake estate business is the fictional work known as the appraisal. The bankers provide the tax-free money largely on the basis of reviewing this piece of fantasy. Real estate borrowers place as much emphasis on who is appraising their property as in who is doing the plumbing work. An example, done on a small scale, follows:

I buy a duplex for $20,000. I put $5,000 down and convince the sellers to take back a mortgage for the balance. The terms of the mortgage allow me to refinance the debt. The sellers agree to this because one of the units is vacant and the duplex has deferred maintenance. I also convince the sellers to allow me access to the property before the closing of the sale.

I immediately start work on the units. I paint the vacant unit, put in new carpeting, take care of neglected landscaping, throw some shingles on the roof. I find a tenant for the vacant unit and sign the current tenant to a new lease. My renovations total $5,000. My total cost is $25,000 but I've actually had to pay out only $10,000.

I find a friendly real estate appraiser and have him visit the property. I tell him about the work I've done and the work I plan to do in the future. I give him compliments on the tie he is wearing and the car he is driving. He in turn gives me an appraised value that is substantially higher than my combined purchase price and renovation cost. The appraisal reports shows a Fair Market Value (a concept which exists only in theory, never in reality) of $45,000. The main factor contributing to this value is the fact that the rental income will support the expenses of the property and the annual debt service.

My next step is to take the appraisal to my local banker. The appraiser is on the approved list for his institution. I'm in luck. The banker gives me a loan based on 80% of the appraised value of the property. Eighty percent of $45,000 equals $36,000. I receive my loan, pay the sellers of the property the $15,000 balance I owe them, deduct my down payment and renovation costs totaling $10,000 and realize a profit of $11,000. Because that amount came to me in the form of a mortgage, it is tax-free.

I take my $11,000 and go out to look for another property that I can put through the same process;each time attempting to find larger properties with a wider spread between the acquisition price and the appraised value that I can create by renovating the property.

This scenario is played out for real every day in America. It is played out using properties as small as my duplex and as large as 500-unit apartment buildings. It is played out with shopping centers and office buildings. It is played out in small town and large cities. It is the driving force behind the entire industry.

That driver's seat is occupied by the real estate developers and the investors. They're the ones who put things into motion that culminate with money being borrowed from banks and other lenders and ending up in more properties, expensive houses and cars, vacation homes, and in support of their life-styles.

There are two types of real estate developers--those who realize how the game is played and those who see themselves as exemplary businessmen providing a great service by taking inflated appraisals to the local bank and walking out with tax-free money. In my experience, the far more interesting characters are the developers who understand that they are playing a game, how the game is played and understand their role and the role of everyone else in the game.

Some of the developers I've worked with and discussed projects with ended up taking the money they were able to separate from lenders and attempted to get into other businesses. I've known developers and real estate investors who tried and failed at becoming Broadway producers, motion picture producers, cable-TV operators, restaurant owners and gym owners. I honestly don't know of any venture that a real estate developer entered into outside of real estate that proved to be successful. My opinion on that matter is that the business of borrowing large amounts of money from banks becomes relatively easy for a real estate developer who knows the process. Those other industries don't have the same easy source of tax-free revenue. Those other industries are highly competitive and require more creativity, ingenuity, intelligence and persistence than is required by the real estate business.

Many real estate people I know, both large and small, were unable to stay in the game or were not allowed to keep playing. Once they started receiving the money from the banks upon the refinancing of properties, they didn't save enough money to maintain their properties. After spending the cash on things other than real estate, they found themselves faced with a shortage of cash when one of their rental properties needed a new roof, furnace, windows, etc. or if there was a period of prolonged vacancy among a high number of the units. One of the most interesting stories concerns a shopping center investor who built himself up to the point where he owned or had management contracts for 17 strip shopping centers. He kept leveraging and leveraging and found himself in a situation where he had a ton of property but little cash. When some of his larger tenants did not renew leases he found himself scrambling to come up with the money to make the mortgage payments. When he could tread water no longer, his empire collapsed like a house of cards. Every one of the properties he owned ended up in foreclosure or sold under fire sale prices, and his management contracts were not renewed. Many people remarked to me about this gentleman's downfall and found delight in his failure. I found the story of his meteoric rise and quick accumulation of square footage just as interesting.

There were other real estate players I knew who became ex-players because they acquired and attempted to refinance that one property that just couldn't get turned around. They came upon the one deal that needed too much renovation, the one deal that did not get leased up and the one deal that couldn't get the appraised value they needed to pull the cash out of a lender. The similarities among these people were they lived large, craved publicity and always bragged about how well they were doing. The ones that kept quiet, realized it was a game they were playing and didn't take on the Waterloo project or didn't over spend their money on a lavish life-style were the ones that were able to stay in the game.

Why should my experiences in the real estate business and my stories of characters from the real estate business be of interest and importance to you?

Because the banks that give the tax-free money to the real estate developers and investors are getting that money from you, your family members, your neighbors and your friends. Your money is going into the pockets of the real estate players to buy their homes, their cars and boats, pay for their vacations, and other personal uses. I doubt people would continue to place money into bank accounts or buy Certificates of Deposit if they knew where the money was going to end up.

Before we continue, let's have a brief review. The return you receive from a deposit into a bank account or CD is roughly equal to the current inflation rate. If that account is not qualified (meaning not in a IRA account), you are paying taxes on the interest you are receiving. After adjusting for taxes and the inflation rate, your return from a bank instrument may bring your real return to below zero.

Do banks or S&Ls ever let you in on what really goes on in their industry? Or what will happen to your purchasing power if you leave your money with them? Absolutely not. Banks require a constant stream of unsophisticated and uninformed individuals putting their money into low-yielding bank accounts, adding a two point spread and then giving the money to a borrower. The marketing and advertising used by the banking industry is among the most offensive and insulting in the financial services industry. I constantly hear bank commercials on the radio attempting to scare investors about the stock market and why market volatility and declines will hurt you. The commercials then implore you to immediately remove your money from the investment vehicle that will provide you with the highest return and put it into the vehicle with the lowest return. Newspaper ads, in large block print, tell you what rate you can get for locking your money up in a 5-year CD while letting you know your money is Federally-insured up to $100,000. Banks also must rely heavily on institutional advertising to get your money. They will use every conceivable means to let you know what great corporate citizens they are, what worthwhile charity work they are involved with and what they are doing to make your neighborhood a better place to live. They tell you everything except what is true: the yield you are receiving on your savings account and CDs will provide you with a net negative return once adjusted for inflation and taxes.

The way commercial banks and savings & loans operate today varies dramatically from the way they both operated for most of their existence. The negative changes that occurred recently have outweighed the positive changes that were implemented by regulators in the past to fix problems that surfaced within the system.

In the decade of the 1920's banks operated with little regulation. Not only were they allowed to invest directly in the stock of corporations, they were allowed to underwrite new stock issues. Banks were also allowed to set the margin rate at whatever percentage they so desired. These facts, coupled together, were major culprits in the bizarre stock market run-up of the late 1920's and part of the reason for the stock market crash. At the time there was no SEC to at least review new stock issues. All stock was unregistered because there was no government body to register it. Because the Federal Reserve did not recognize the importance of the margin rate on stock prices, banks were allowed to set the rate wherever they wanted. Today the margin rate is 50% (this means that an investor can purchase $1,000 worth of stock by investing $500 and borrowing the other $500. Brokerage houses make a commission on the stock sale and interest income on the $500 loan). In the months leading to October 1929 banks were allowing investors to purchase $1,000 worth of stock by investing only $100 and borrowing the remaining $900. Not only were banks making money on the margin loans, they were making commission income from the new stock issues they were selling and capital gains from the inflated prices of the stocks they held in their own portfolios.

But all good (?) things must come to an end. When the air started to leak out of the artificially inflated stock market balloon that the banks helped to create, the prices of stocks plummeted. Banks were doing the same thing every investor was doing in the days after October 29, 1929--selling high priced/low value stock issues into a declining market. They were also attempting to make margin calls on investors whose margin accounts were decimated by the declining prices. Of course, those investors didn't have the cash to pay off the loans the banks had given them. Investors gladly gave back the stock issues in lieu of making cash payments but by the time those issues were assigned to the banks they were worthless.

When the dust settled after the market crash, the government created the Securities and Exchange Commission to regulate the investment industry. The government also passed the Glass-Steagall Act which separated commercial banking from investment banking and barred banks from selling securities. The government then gave the banking industry a big crutch by providing deposit insurance of $25,000. Even though the behavior of banks was in large part responsible for the market bubble and subsequent bust of 1929, Congress gave them a tool that in essence would be used into the future to hide the mistakes of poor management and inefficient operations in addition to becoming a great marketing tool that enabled them to attract low rate deposits. *(I will refer you again to John Kenneth Galbraith's The Great Crash, 1929 for more detailed information on the role banks played in the stock market crash.)*

Savings and loans were originally chartered with the idea of providing residential mortgages to facilitate home ownership in America. S&Ls were first owned by the depositors in the form of 'mutual' institutions. The pooling of minor amounts of money enabled the members of the institution to afford home ownership. Each member, or depositor, was helping their fellow depositors attain low rate financing on their home.

But both types of institutions operate today much differently than their intended purpose. The high interest rates of the early 1980's wrecked the theory upon which the banking industry was built. That theory held that financial institutions could sell you a CD at 5% and lend me money at 7%. When rates shot up, bankers found themselves with 7% mortgages and a market that was demanding 12% Certificates of Deposit. Later, banks and S&Ls found themselves losing literally billions of dollars to the mutual fund industry.

The banking industry did what any industry does that cannot compete anymore. They cried to Congress for relief from the competition. The insurance on deposit accounts was increased to $100,000 in 1980. Banks are allowed to own subsidiaries dealing in securities once again. They can also sell mutual funds inside their branch offices along with insurance products. Glass-Steagall, which was installed to protect the public from stock speculation of banks, is now dead.

S&Ls were allowed to establish service companies which allowed them to own real estate and make direct investments into other ventures. Their regulating body, the Federal Home Loan Bank Board, also allowed loans to be made on commercial property and, in the mid-1980's, made it easier to obtain a charter to start a S&L owned by stockholders instead of the traditional mutual form of ownership. And that is when the fun began.

For all the descriptive phrases I can use to describe the real estate developers I've met, the one phrase I can use among the more successful ones is this: they are smart people. They can grasp the complexities of a deal quickly, they know when they are being hyped or scammed by brokers and fellow developers, and they know how to deal with lenders.

I cannot say the same thing about people who work in the banking industry. As a group, they are among the least intelligent people I've come across in the world of business. When they were allowed to advance from making residential loans to commercial loans, the real estate developers licked their chops. There was no way these bankers were mentally equipped to deal with the real estate sharks who had been devouring more sophisticated lenders for years. The S&Ls became the private piggy banks of the real estate profession. New buildings were built that had no business being put into the ground and existing buildings were sold at astronomical prices, all because the developers and investors could borrow far more money than any project was worth. If the rents did not cover the expenses and the mortgage payments, so what? The loans were given without any personal signatures. If the project failed, the developers and investors kept the money and turned the keys to the front door over to the particular S&L that was unfortunate enough to have made the loan.

When it became easy to obtain a charter to open a S&L, the real estate developers became lenders. With the insurance of deposits, they were able to attract money by offering high rates on Certificates of Deposit and then use the money to finance the projects of their friends. When too much money came in the front door in response to high rates and couldn't be put into real estate deals fast enough, the lenders bought CDs at other newly opened S&Ls. *(I once had to invest $8,000,000 into CDs and I had two days to do it. Because I could not put more than $100,000 into any one institution because of insurance limitations, I found myself wiring money to S&Ls across the country. We were still in the period of high inflation and it was before the S&L scandal was revealed. The average yield I obtained when the last of the money had been wired was 11.50%).*

The combination of unprepared and ill-equipped old-time lenders trying to make loans on commercial projects and the ease of getting charters to open stockholder-owned S&Ls was directly responsible for the S&L scandal and the accompanying criminal activity. Instead of using taxpayer money to resurrect the industry, Congress should have done what the marketplace was telling it to do...let the industry shrink down to the size that the magic force of supply and demand wanted it to be. Instead, the industry received even more assistance from Congress and only a small fraction of the culprits who were responsible for raping S&Ls received the punishment their crimes deserved.

Banks and S&Ls will face a major problem in the future. Much of their asset base is deposits held in low-interest bearing accounts. There is an estimated $1.2 trillion in passbook savings accounts and money market accounts. Much of this money is owned by senior citizens who were never taught that the interest they are getting from the bank is approximately equal to the inflation rate plus the tax rate. They were also never taught what happens to their money once the low-yielding account is opened.

When those senior citizens pass away, their more sophisticated children and grandchildren will remove the funds from the bank accounts and invest it in the stock market. As they make their way to the front door of the bank or S&L branch, they will be stopped by a woman or man jumping up from a tin desk. This person will be the in-house investment broker working for, or on behalf of, the bank. The fact that banks and S&Ls can now sell mutual funds directly to their depositors completes the cycle that started when Congress barred banks from participating in the underwriting and selling of securities because of their pre-October 1929 behavior and their involvement in the stock market bubble and burst. The banking industry had to lobby to have Glass-Steagall eliminated because they were losing billions of dollars of deposits to the mutual fund industry and, with inflation under control, would continue to do so.

As objective and unbiased as I can be, I am going to share my knowledge of banks and S&Ls selling investment products. The broker who is working inside the branches, occupying the desk next to the tellers, is an investment professional who most likely could not survive in the industry without the depositors walking over to his/her desk after being steered there by one of the tellers. They are people who were able to obtain a license to sell investment products, but the intricacies of the business--asset allocation, management fees, portfolio turnover rates, down markets--escape them. They would most likely not be able to survive in the industry if they didn't have the immediate referral of investors. In a sense, they are my competitors. But if they had to deal beyond their client base of uninformed and unaware individuals, they would provide no competition to me.

One of the major reasons they are not competition is the quality of products they offer. When banks started to make allegiances with mutual fund managers, the successful and well established mutual fund managers didn't need to be, or wanted to be, purchased by a banking entity. The banks could only partner with companies that needed the life support a bank or S&L could offer. In my city, two large banks, PNC and Mellon, partnered with mutual fund companies that were tired and old fixed-income managers that were at risk of fading away. Because the continued low inflation decreased the demand for bonds, these fund companies were losing assets. After they were acquired or partnered with the bank, the fund companies started offering stock mutual funds. This was similar to the point in time when S&Ls were allowed to start making commercial loans after decades of doing nothing but residential loans. The number of people doing it, and doing it well, was a barrier to entry. The performance of the bank-owned or controlled mutual funds has lagged behind the performance of the properly run mutual funds. One of the fund companies that was acquired by a Pittsburgh bank was fined heavily by the SEC for manipulation of one of their stock funds. They misrepresented the yield of the fund and then marketed the false return heavily as a way to attract more investors.

It is easy for me to teach clients why they should have only minimal money in a bank or savings & loan. I tell them about declining purchasing power and the low rates paid by banks, I tell them what the bank will be doing with their money and I tell them the history of banks and the securities industry.

I started this essay with details of my love/hate relationship with the real estate business. I want to conclude it with two insights into that business and a story that summarizes my feelings about the industry.

The real estate business was where I was first taught to separate fact from fiction and where I learned that there is a range of people not telling the truth. This talent has served me well in the investment and healthcare businesses and in my personal life. I will forever be grateful for the lessons I learned in determining the value of information and the credibility of people giving me that information.

I have tremendous knowledge of the true workings of the real estate business. I know how the game is played. I know the personalities involved;I know what the true value of a piece of property is and I know how to embellish that value so that a lender will give me far more money that the property is worth. If I had so chosen, I could have been an extremely successful real estate developer/investor. I like to think that I developed a higher purpose in life and that I obtained more important goals than to take advantage of the banking industry and the mediocre people employed by it.

I made reference earlier to the pool hall my grandfather operated in the South Side of Pittsburgh. When I was young and visiting my grandparents' house, I would often walk two blocks to the small shopping center close to their house. There was a supermarket and four smaller tenants in this center. In front of the supermarket an older gentleman would set up a table and sell soft pretzels out of wicker baskets. This gentleman was a fixture at the center.

Years later, when I got my job in the real estate development business, my boss bought this very shopping center. The supermarket had moved to a larger, newer location and the smaller tenants had turned over a few times. The supermarket was still under lease, and they were operating a bulk foods store in the location. Their lease called for them to pay "pass-throughs" (pro rated increases in real estate taxes, insurance and utility charges over a base year). The previous owners had never billed the supermarket chain. My assignment was to determine the amount of money the supermarket owed and prepare a bill.

One day I took a drive to this property that I had not visited for years. Much to my surprise I noticed an older man selling pretzels in front of the doors to the supermarket. I walked over and bought two pretzels and realized it was the same man who sold me pretzels when I was a young boy.

The next day my boss came into my office. As a combination of wanting to share a unique story with another human and to advance our working relationship, I told my boss that the same man who sold pretzels when I was a kid was still there selling them.

My boss looked at me and said, "The same guy who sold pretzels to you was in front of the store yesterday? And he was selling pretzels?"

Thinking that he realized the interesting aspect of this story, I told him that it was true. My boss looked at me for a moment and then said: *"How much rent do you think we can get out of him?"*

True story. And the story that best describes my experiences in, and the inside workings of, the real estate business.

Thinking About Money

A few years ago I met with a potential client. He was a hard-working owner of a beer distributorship. He told me had invested $20,000 into a junk bond mutual fund two years previously and his investment was now worth $14,000. I explained to him how interest rate increases have a negative correlation with the value of bonds and that some of the bonds in the portfolio could have defaulted which would have further reduced the value of his investment. I also told him that this was the improper type of investment for a person his age and with his investment objective.

A look of partial understanding came over his face. I told him what the proper investment vehicles would be, why they were proper for him and discussed the fee structures and turnover rates. I then told him he should move his money from the junk bond fund and put it into the mutual fund combination I had recommended.

He told me he was going to call the broker who sold him the junk bond fund and redeem his shares. He would put it into the asset allocation I suggested for him--just as soon as the investment returned to the $20,000 level. When I told him that the investment most likely would never return to that level and reiterated the reasons why, the look of understanding disappeared.

He was set on getting out of that investment the amount he put in. My knowledge of bonds and stocks and interest rates at that time wasn't complete enough to convince him to take the loss, learn the lesson, and invest in the proper allocation. He was married to that junk bond fund with a no-divorce agreement. He eventually became a client and took his money out of that junk bond fund, but it took some creative teaching on my part to convince him that his investment would probably never be worth $20,000 again.

I have noticed other situations like this. People making improper investments and then being unable to separate themselves from the investment. One of my clients owns a mutual fund with a value that declines each year. She keeps this fund because her nephew, who lasted about two months in the investment business as a broker, sold it to her. Other clients have loaded up their portfolios with the stock of their employer and suffered tremendous losses when the value and the price of that stock went down.

I also deal with people on a regular basis who express to me an interest in learning about investment analysis and the proper way to invest money. These people are supplied with material I've written and information on the mutual fund company I use. When I see them again or call as a follow-up, the response I get is that they've been too busy to review the material or they have read only one page of a three-page article.

The behavior described above, and other similar seemingly irrational behavior, can all be explained by the growing field of behavioral economics. The understanding of human behavior learned through the study of psychology has been applied to the world of finance to gain a better understanding of why investors make the decisions they do and why they take or don't take the course of action that seems to contain the most common sense and is the most prudent. The Bible of this field of study is titled *Why Smart People Make Big Money Mistakes*. The authors are Gary Belsky and Thomas Gilovich. Belsky is a highly regarded business journalist with an unparalleled resume. Gilovich is a professor of psychology at Cornell University and the author of numerous research papers on psychology and the human decision-making process. Their combined effort produced a book that is a must-read for anybody in and out of the investment business.

There are few subjects, and perhaps only one, that touch as many human emotions as the subject of money. The only other thing I know that can simultaneously cause humans to experience stress and happiness, misery and elation, anguish and contentment in the same way that finances can is romance. And if you think about it, many great romances are ended, altered or never started because of issues related to money.

The authors of the book detailed many instances in which behavioral economics affects our spending and investment habits. I saw myself in the passage about consumers who will pay more for a product or service when buying by credit instead of cash and in the section about buyers who will pay for ancillary items, such as service agreements, when buying a large item. When we are paying $25,000 for a new automobile, we may spend an additional $2,000 for a stereo or $1,000 to upgrade the wheels. If we were given the choice of paying these amounts for the items separately, there is no way we would make the purchase. Because we're looking at a $25,000 purchase, we value the ancillary items in a different manner.

Some of the psychological profiles identified in the book are listed below and summarized for your review. The first two deal with every day buying behavior.

THE ANCHORING THEORY--This occurs when we tie a price to a certain object, even though the price may have an invalid rationale. We center our decision around this price. The best example is the concept of engagement rings. The rule of thumb is that a man interested in asking for a girl's hand in marriage should spend two months salary for the ring. This rule of thumb was most likely developed and hyped by the jewelry industry as a way to increase their revenue. More realistic advice on what should be spent for an engagement ring is what the buyer can afford *(other factors are his age and how many times he and his intended have previously gone shopping for engagement rings with other people).*

THE ENDOWMENT THEORY--People often place more value into what they currently own than the alternatives. The theory is widely used by any company that sells you a product with a "money back guarantee." The seller of the product realizes that buyers will most times develop a certain allegiance to a product they buy. Even if not totally satisfied, as the ads will say, people tend to place this allegiance over the idea of getting a refund. The second part of this theory, developed by me, is that people are too lazy to re-wrap a product that doesn't do what it was advertised to do, fill out the required paperwork, and take it to the Post Office to return it.

The following examples of investor behavior are directly related to the investment business.

THE SUNK COST THEORY--The term "throwing good money after bad" describes this theory. It is present in all businesses to some degree. People and companies become too emotionally attached to an investment, or they won't admit they made a mistake by originally financing the venture. They continue to finance the investment or venture even though their objectivity or common sense tells them to walk away.

THE DISPOSITION THEORY--Investors have a tendency to hold on to their bad investments for too long and sell their good investments too soon. For the first part of this theory, think about my client with the $14,000 in the junk bond fund waiting for it to climb back to his magic exit point of $20,000. If I hadn't found a way to convince him to get closure with his loss and move the money into the proper mutual fund for his objective, he would still be losing money inside that junk bond fund. The second part is carried out each trading day by investors who think they are smarter than the market and who sell out of stocks with increasing value. Unfortunately, much of that selling is motivated by brokers who are making money for themselves by moving clients' money from one investment to another and by charging "wrap-fees" on the account value. Some of these brokers feel they have to do something--even if it is the wrong thing--to justify the increased fees they are charging.

THE CONFIRMATION BASIS THEORY--People often make investments using an irrational decision-making process and continue to hold that investment even though it provides no value to their portfolio. The authors of the book gave an example of a person who bought a stock because it was recommended to him by a well-known individual. Even though the stock decreased in value immediately and never turned around, that person will not sell because of the connection to the celebrity who gave the recommendation. My client who continues to hold the mutual fund sold to them by a nephew is another example of this theory.

THE HERD MENTALITY THEORY--This occurs when people let others determine the value of an item for them, often times with assistance from the media. A person with good common sense and intelligence may throw that common sense to the side if enough people they come in contact with are buying an investment. Examples of this profile can be found throughout history and most recently with the great NASDAQ market bubble and burst of 1998 to 2000.

The following profiles have been developed by me from my experiences dealing with investors and non-investors during my stay in the business.

THE 'NO DECISION IS MY DECISION' CLIENT--I see this one almost every day. People who do not have a basic knowledge of investments and refuse to learn cross my path on a regular basis. They have the wrong asset allocation, are paying excessive management fees, suffer from high turnover rates and their money is not working for them. But they are in such fear of the investment business they cannot bring themselves to take another look at their investment plan. The decision-making process behind the money they originally invested caused them so much stress and anguish that they don't want to experience those feelings again. They would rather stay invested improperly than suffer the negative feelings that they now associate with finances. *The cure for those feelings is for these people to face their fears, learn about the business, and turn a stress into a strength.*

THE "I'M TOO BUSY" CLIENT--This is somewhat related to the profile above. I have supplied numerous clients, in all income and age ranges, with information on investing. This material ranges from essays and articles I've written to pieces prepared by a mutual fund family. When I make a follow-up phone call, most people tell me they have been too busy to read a three-page article. From my own observation it turns out that the individuals with the most wealth and the busiest schedules are the people that do read the material. It is the group of people with the less demanding job or profession and the lower asset base that tells me how busy they are and that they couldn't find ten minutes to read an article.

THE "DON'T SHOOT THE MESSENGER" CLIENT--Once people realize their investment portfolio is structured improperly and that there are better alternatives, they often do not make any changes. By keeping their portfolio as is, they compound one problem with another. I think by making the change to the proper allocation they will develop feelings of regret due to the time they wasted (and the money they lost) by not being invested properly. People who fit this profile sometimes look at me as the bearer of bad news and cast a negative light over me once I show them the proper way.

THE "REAL VS. NOMINAL RETURN" CLIENT--There are many people who do not understand that a dollar invested today is worth more than a dollar not invested today. This is one of the difficulties in signing up workers to participate in a 401(k) program. This theory also holds that people don't understand what inflation does to money in bank accounts and what their opportunity cost is--the money they don't make because they are invested in assets that only keep pace, or barely beat, the inflation rate.

There is currently over $1.2 trillion in bank savings accounts and money market accounts. These are among the lowest, if not the lowest, yielding investment vehicles being marketed to consumers. Much of that dollar amount is in accounts controlled by people who fit one of the profiles listed above. Ignorance is not bliss, especially when it comes to the investment business.

The investment community has known about investor psychology for a long time. That is why the characters in the investment business I presented throughout this book do the things they do. The brokers who go to various churches and appear on the Christian radio stations know that by making a religious connection in the minds of potential clients they achieve a certain acceptance. The broker who leased the Porsche 944 probably found some silly person to give him money because of the car. There was at least one person, I'm sure, to equate that car, and the person driving it, with knowledge and ability in the investment business. Too bad the broker didn't show his car to enough people. He might have been able to make enough commissions to keep up the lease payments.

The way brokers dress, how they decorate their offices, the publications they leave on the table in the waiting area, the Holiday Inn seminars, and the radio call-in shows are all done for one reason--to get potential clients to like or trust the broker even before they meet them. It doesn't matter if the broker charges excessive fees or doesn't have a grasp of the topics presented in Part Two of this book. My business, like most businesses, is a business of marketing. And a good marketing effort will overcome a lack of knowledge, high priced/low valued investments and an improperly structured asset allocation.

I remember the insurance agent who sold insurance to my parents. He came to the house during evening hours always dressed in a suit and tie, even during the summer months. He was slick, polished and spoke with such confidence you would have thought he invented the very policies he was selling. I'm sure he sold my parents insurance they did not need. I'm sure there were policies that would have been less expensive that would have served the same purpose, and I'm sure my parents didn't fully understand what they were buying. But whatever he was selling, they bought it.

People must buy things differently today than they did in previous generations. The information explosion is here, and it will not go away. There is easy access to impartial and objective information on any subject. Consumers of investment products, insurance policies, automobiles, medical services, travel services, etc., have access to the information they need to have in order to level the playing field with the marketers of those and every other product and service.

Salespeople will not be able to rely on their "Willy Loman" skills in the future. They will have to become more like educators than closers. Consumers will be smarter, so the people selling goods and services will have to be smarter. Marketers will have to find more effective and efficient ways to teach their buyers about the value of the product or service they are selling. And if the product has no or limited value, the marketplace will find that out and dismiss that product or service from the marketplace.

It is now time for the buyers to understand how investor psychology affects their buying, and investment, decisions. Level the playing field. Read *Why Smart People Make Big Money Mistakes.* I identified myself in at least three sections of this book, and I identified clients and non-clients in other sections. That book should become part of your library--right next to this one.

E S S A Y S

"What does Bob 'The Gunner' Prince have in common with the U.S. stock market?"

L ike many kids, a large part of my young life was devoted to baseball. I played baseball whenever or wherever possible (my father spray painted bases in the cul-de-sac in front of our house), bounced a rubber ball against the blocks of my parents' house if there were no other kids around to pick up a game, had a sliding pit in my backyard and listened to Pittsburgh Pirates' radio broadcasts on my transistor radio.

I have strong memories of listening to the Pirates' play-by-play man, Bob "The Gunner" Prince, announcing the games, and I especially looked forward to the games played on the West Coast. It was during these games that I would fall asleep while listening to Mr. Prince's unique phrases and unbridled bias toward the Pirates

Of all the sayings, expressions and stories The Gunner told, I remember in great detail his concept of the "Hidden Vigorish." The Hidden Vig was applied in the following manner: if a team on their way into town to play the Pirates was on a nine game winning streak, Mr. Prince had a way to convince me not to worry. "The longer they keep winning games, they closer they are to losing a game," Prince would say, most likely between sips of Iron City beer. Or if Roberto Clemente was in a 0-19 batting slump, there was no need to be concerned. "The longer Roberto goes without getting a hit, the closer he is to getting a hit," Prince would tell me over the radio and ensure a peaceful night of sleep for me.

What does this have to do with the U.S. stock market and investment analysis? As it turns out, the answer is "a great deal."

Bob Prince may not have been an expert in the field of Probability & Statistics, but he was an expert in the winning percentages of baseball teams and batting averages of baseball players. What he was doing was charting the results of events that occurred over "statistically significant" periods of time and applying them to the near future performance of baseball players and teams. As history revealed, the team with the nine game winning streak eventually lost a game (like most teams, about as many as they won) and Roberto Clemente eventually did get a hit (actually 3,000 of them).

If we examine the "statistically significant" results of the U.S. stock market, we learn that the overall market has finished with a negative return in 31 of the 98 years (*in baseball parlance: an inverse .316 batting average*) since the beginning of the century (Source: DJIA and Ibbotson Large Company Index). Since 1926 the number of months the market has finished with a negative return has been approximately 40%.

We have not had a year with a negative return in the Dow Jones Industrial Index since 1990. In order for the "Hidden Vig" to work, the previous seven years with positive returns will be offset with at least two years of negative returns. Add to the mix that many stocks are trading at historic P/E ratio highs and numerous stock prices have increased without the companies' having increased the underlying assets or earnings to support the prices. The next negative year or years of the U.S. market could be substantial declines. Equity index funds will be among the fastest falling investment objectives during the next market decline for two reasons. They do not have the ability to change their objective once the underlying stocks start to decline.

These funds also have minimal cash for redemptions and will have to sell shares into a declining market in order to return cash to the investors who will requesting their money back.

The Mathematics of Loss
The statistical analysis of loss provides interesting insight into what can happen to Average Annual Returns after a negative return. As an example: if a portfolio earned 10% a year for three years and then had a negative return of 10% in year four, the AAR over four years is 4.6%. In order to achieve an AAR of 10% for five years, the portfolio will have to earn **34.4%** in the fifth year. This exercise shows that one negative year has the ability to severely impact three consecutive positive years at a much faster rate than it took the portfolio to grow.

Protection Against Down Markets
A properly structured retirement, pension or individual portfolio has built-in protection against down markets. These protections include proper asset allocation, low annual fees, low portfolio turnover rates and diversification into international markets.

Asset allocation determines the overall performance of any portfolio. Many investors, with short memories and being poor students of stock market history, began to invest heavily in the stock market after seeing the above average returns achieved over the last four years. The problem is a portion of this money has a short-term use (retirement, tuition, business expansion, etc.). A market downturn will alter their plans dramatically.

When the stock market is achieving double digit returns, a high management fee can be absorbed. But when the return is single digit or negative, that excessive management fee will still be coming out of the assets, causing further erosion to the asset base. Many investors are paying excessive management fees and other fees on their assets. Individual investors should get rid of "wrap" fees, "rebalancing" fees and the other excessive fees so popular among brokers. Business clients should unbundle their "packaged" retirement plans to ensure the most efficient fee structure on Profit-sharing/401(k) plans.

A high portfolio turnover rate is a symptom of poor investment research. A high turnover rate also adds additional fees known as transaction costs to portfolios. This is the cost incurred by an asset manager to buy and sell securities. The average portfolio turnover rate for a stock mutual fund is 86%. This type of turnover can add as much as 50 basis points to the fee structure of a mutual fund. A high turnover rate may also be linked to inconsistency of management.

The U.S. market is rarely, if ever, the leading equity market. Proper diversification allows investors to receive equity-type returns without exposing themselves to the risk of being overly invested in one market. (One related note: developing countries have 84% of the world's population, 50% of the world's economy and 15% of the stock market value. It is imprudent for a long-term investor not to have exposure to developing countries).

Lastly, Warren Buffett, whose connection to this essay is that he is the owner of a minor league baseball team, had a great quote about the next declining stock market. Mr. Buffett said, "When the tide goes out, we'll see who's been swimming naked."

Make sure you are prepared for the next low tide.

/s/ Kenneth Kaszak
Registered Representative
August 1999

How *NOT* To Choose a
Pension Plan Manager

It's always been a source of interest (and amusement) to see what criteria companies use when choosing their qualified plan asset manager and/or plan administrator. As stated in a previous newsletter, many people who start or run businesses are experts in their fields, but when it comes to selecting a plan manager, they just don't know which variables are valid and reliable and which are irrelevant and simply a part of the sales process.

Here are a few of the wrong reasons to select a qualified plan manager:

"The Trade Group Endorsement" Many businesses choose their plan manager because of an endorsement from their trade group. These businesses mistakenly believe the endorsement was based on objective decision-making ability inside the trade group offices. What these businesses don't realize is this: Most trade associations are run by professional administrators, people removed from the day-to-day activity of running a business and making decisions based on value, cost and long term impact. The information these administrators think is

relevant and valid is often diversionary information offered to them as part of the sales pitch. The important criteria for structuring a qualified savings plan will not change but remains a mystery to many trade group employees. They just don't know which variables they need to study before making a recommendation to trade group members.

"The Consultant Recommendation" My experience dealing with consultants who hold themselves out as experts in advising plan sponsors on asset management selection has revealed two items:

1.) Consultants often make their recommendation based on investment results generated over time periods that are invalid or non-relevant. *(Consultants will advise clients to switch to a different manager based on the last 1, 3 or 5 year performance of that manager. These time periods are not statistically significant periods when gauging the performance of a fund manager. The most relevant time periods to use are "Rolling Ten Year Periods" or "Rolling Five Year Periods", i.e. 1988-1998, 1989-1999, etc. or 1993-1998, 1994-1999).* Rolling periods eliminate aberrational years, account for changes in management style and ability, and reveal the asset managers with consistent, superior long-term results. Switching asset managers based on any shorter time horizon results in the consultant, and the plan sponsor, chasing "yesterday's heros."

2.) Consultants add another level of fees to the process, including higher transaction costs, which reduces the growth potential of the portfolio. Extra fees weigh down a portfolio and present an obstacle for the magic of compounded growth. *(Always remember: The Law of Compounded Growth will never be repealed).*

"The Bank Connection" The reasons why banks were not al-

lowed in the securities industry for decades were all valid and relevant. *(See John Kenneth Galbraith's The Great Crash, 1929 for insight into the role banks played in the 1929 crash).* Now that Glass-Steagall Act is becoming a memory and banks are once again allowed to market securities, here's what qualified plan sponsors should know when it comes to banks marketing investment products:

1.) The investment managers that banks have acquired or merged with to date were companies that were "on sale." These investment managers needed to be acquired or enter into a merger because they were losing assets to the more established, more successful independent asset managers. The asset managers who made allegiances with banks were for the most part older fixed-income managers with either zero growth or a continuing loss in assets.

2.) Banks who grant business loans or lines of credit to corporate borrowers in exchange for the borrower turning over its qualified plan assets are skirting with a violation of anti-trust law by tying the loan to the plan assets. Plan sponsors who place plan assets with a bank in order to get the line of credit are in violation of ERISA Rule 401(a)(4), the "Exclusive Purpose Rule." Pension plan liability is the fastest growing area of the legal profession. If a plan sponsor trades its plan assets for a line of credit, it may be in violation of its fiduciary responsibility. If the plan performs poorly, there will be no shortage of attorneys lining up to represent the plan participants.

3.) There isn't a salesperson working for a bank who can compete with an investment professional who is equipped with an in-depth knowledge of the history and mechanics of the capital markets, the importance of asset allocation, the true meaning of the word "risk" and the impact of high management fees and portfolio turnover rates. The asset managers that an objective investment professional works with are better managers that the "captive" managers that a bank employee must work with.

"The Celebrity Salesperson" I have a friend who is well-trained and well-versed in pension plan structure and ERISA regulations. He once told me he lost a trucking company's 401(k) plan to a broker who used to be a member of the Pittsburgh Steelers. (This ex-player had also been involved with two businesses that filed for bankruptcy protection). The plan offered by the former player had higher fees and an asset manager with a track record less attractive than the one offered by my friend. When my friend asked the business owner why he would choose an obviously inferior plan, the business owner replied that he just wanted to do business with somebody who played for the Steelers.

"The In-Law Connection" I used to know a local shopping center developer. He complained to me about the low return on his investment portfolio and the high fees he was paying. When I asked who his broker was, he told me it was his brother-in-law. I suggested that hiring an investment manager simply because he was related was not the most prudent thing to do. The developer agreed with me and told me he knew it wasn't a good idea to hire his brother-in-law...*but that his wife thought it was a great idea!*

Speaking of in-laws, here's a related story. A few years ago I took over the management of a Profit-sharing plan for a small distribution company. They had about $1 million in assets but an improper asset allocation (they were invested 1/3 equally in cash, bonds and stocks). I reallocated their assets, lowered their expenses and provided the company president detailed information on the true workings of the investment business.

Two years later the plan was worth over $1.5 million (without the company making any more contributions). One day, I received a phone call from the president and was told that they were moving the assets away from my management and placing them with the son-in-law of a friend of the company owner. (The son-in-law had just gotten a job with an insurance company). I informed the company president that the insurance company in question was notorious for its high fees, low returns and was the subject of numerous lawsuits from investors. I also told him that "president's friend's son-in-law" was not proper investment manager criteria and that his company may face a future liability issue based on the improper criteria. The company president thanked me for my service and the dramatic increase in assets. I ended the conversation by telling the president that if I ever get to the point where I must rely on in-laws for clients that I will leave the investment business, dig out my work boots, and go back to pouring concrete. *(Note: the insurance company involved recently set aside $3 billion to settle claims filed by aggrieved clients. The son-in-law is probably out of the business).*

/s/ Kenneth Kaszak
Registered Representative
July 1999

Unwrap Your Packaged Retirement Plan

Evidence is strong for "unbundling" of qualified savings plans

D o you know what a "packaged plan" is? Do you know if your company's plan is packaged or unbundled? If not, don't feel bad. Many plan sponsors are unaware of what they are and the obstacles they present to the growth of a plan's assets.

A packaged plan is a qualified plan that combines the asset management and plan administration under one wrapped fee. The fee is a percentage of the plan assets. Brokers (oftentimes working for an insurance company) or sales people working for a bank sell packaged plans to business owners and CFOs by pitching the convenience of wrapped plans. If the plan your company has is packaged, you are paying heavily for this convenience, which really isn't a convenience, as you'll soon see.

The most effective and efficient way to structure a plan is to separate the asset management from the plan's administration requirements and pay each vendor according to the value of the services they provide. If you don't do this...if you wrap your plan...it will cost your company in two ways:

NUMBER ONE

The annual fee deducted from a packaged plan is much higher than a separated plan. This results in a hurdle to the growth of the plan's assets. (Remember: The "Law of Compounded Growth" will never be repealed). A few examples follow:

Say your Profit-sharing/401(k) plan has $1,000,000 in assets and your plan has 25 participants. You are paying 1.5% of the plan's assets per year to have the assets managed and the paperwork monitored. *(This fee is on the low side. Many packaged plans charge in excess of 2%)*. Your plan is being charged $15,000 per year. The same plan, after removing the expensive packaging, should pay no more than 75 basis points (3/4 of 1%) per year for asset management or $7,500. The administration cost (which includes all required bookkeeping, preparation of IRS Form 5500, quarterly processing and semi-annual discrimination testing would cost $3,545. The total cost of the un-bundled plan would be $11,025.

Let's look at the same plan with $2,000,000 in assets. If it were packaged with a fee of 1.5% it would pay $30,000 in annual fees. If the asset management were separated from the paperwork the cost would be $18,525. ($3,525 in administration plus $15,000 in asset management. At $3,000,000 the packaged plan is paying $45,000 yearly while the unpackaged plan is paying a total of $26,025. At $4,000,000 the respective annual charges are $60,000 and $33,525. The difference equals a major (and unnecessary) expense for record keeping and data entry, most of which is made simple through the use of computer programs. *(It is ironic that many companies who pay these excessive charges utilize computers every day in their businesses or are themselves part of the computer industry)*.

Let's take a look at the "opportunity cost" of a packaged plan. At the $4,000,000 level the difference in fees equals $26,475. If that money stayed in the plan (instead of being paid out in fees) and continued to grow tax-deferred at the rate of 12% annually, the additional Future Value of the plan in 10 years would be **$82,227** and **$255,385** in 20 years.

There is a positive correlation between high fees and low rates of return for investment portfolios (see Morningstar Monitor's "Expenses Kill"). Paying prudent fees for asset management and administration is part of the line-up for proper plan structure. The other components are proper asset allocation, low portfolio turnover rates, selecting an asset manager with proprietary research ability and above average performance in down markets, and continuous employee education programs that are both relevant and responsive.

NUMBER TWO

A packaged plan is using plan assets to pay for the bookkeeping. As we demonstrated, this slows down the growth of the assets. If you have an unbundled plan, you can use deductible corporate dollars to pay for the administration. Not only does this result in much lower plan fees (and greater value for your plan), it provides a minor tax break for the deductible expense. (Insurance companies and brokers who push packaged plans live well off the excessive fees they charge their clients).

THE BOTTOM LINE: Packaged retirement plans result in excessive Profit-sharing/401(k) fees and decreased value to the plan. This fact of investment life is only now starting to become widely known in the industry...although insurance companies and banks who sell packaged plans would rather keep it hidden.

THE BOTTOM LINE (PART II): People reading this essay have numerous demands on their time and energy during the day. The topic of qualified plans is often relegated to a less than important status. But because of the significance and long term impact of this issue, along with recent changes in liability issues, I would like to see business owners and managers devote a small amount of high-reward time to the issue. Once you learn the mechanics of the capital markets, the impact of high fees and turnover rates on yields and proper plan structure, the fundamentals of investment analysis will become as comfortable to you as the industry-specific lingo, data and facts utilized in your business on a day-to-day basis (and provide you with great insight for your personal investment portfolio).

/s/ Kenneth Kaszak
Registered Representative
November 1999

THE 'DIRTY DOZEN'

Top Twelve Mistakes Made by Pension Plan Sponsors
(with apologies to Lee Marvin, Charles Bronson,
Jim Brown, Ernest Borgnine, et. al.)

1. IMPROPER ASSET ALLOCATION

Number 1 this year, last year and every year. How important is asset allocation? The SEI Corporation, a $600 billion global money management firm, performed a 20-year study of 90 investment portfolios. The result: 93% of a portfolio's performance is correlated to its allocation and 7% is correlated to individual securities selection and/or market timing. Complying with the remainder of this list will not mean a thing if your portfolio is outside of the proper asset allocation range.

2. EXCESSIVE MANAGEMENT FEES

Only now are we beginning to understand the adverse impact of high management fees. Over the last twelve months numerous business publications, in addition to the SEC and Princeton University, have published studies detailing the adverse effects of high management fees on investment portfolios. My own study revealed the following: if we compared two portfolios of $1,000,000 each w/ Plan A paying 75 basis points annually for management and Plan

B paying 1.5% (and each Plan earning 12% per year), Plan A would have $1,168,000 more than Plan B at the end of Year 20.

3. PACKAGING ASSET MANAGEMENT W/ PLAN ADMINISTRATION

Unless your plan has minimal assets, this always results in excessive fees and has earned many insurance brokers a nice income, at the expense of your plan's growth potential. Pay a plan administrator a flat fee and your plan won't become Plan B. You will also be able to deduct administration costs as a business expense.

4. PLAN SPONSORS DON'T UNDERSTAND THE CONCEPT OF RISK

The risk of losing purchasing power, interest rate risk, non-diversification risk and inflation risk are all part of the definition of "risk" and must be considered when a pension plan portfolio is being structured.

5. 401(K) EMPLOYEE EDUCATION PROGRAMS ARE WEAK

Companies aren't doing a proper job of teaching workers the history and mechanics of the capital markets. The proof: 82% of people in 401(k) plans are less than 50 years of age yet only 19% of 401(k) money is invested in equities. Remember: better education and communication programs would result in higher participation by the rank & file which will make the plan more valuable to the owners and key employees.

6. TOO MUCH CASH

Cash and liquidity mean two different things. Inflation has averaged 3.1% over the last 68 years, 4.2% over the last 41 years and 5.8% over the last 21 years. You don't need excess cash to maintain liquidity;and returns from a cash equivalent account, once adjusted for inflation, aren't so impressive.

7. SPONSORS DON'T TAKE ADVANTAGE OF THEIR SIZE

If your plan has $1,000,000 in assets, or is close to that number, you have certain economies of scale you can utilize. These economies come in the form of quality of management, investment cost and management fees. A $1,000,000 plan should not be managed like a $100,000 plan.

8. SPONSORS SELECT MONEY MANAGERS IMPROPERLY

Selecting an asset manager based on their last 1-year to 2-year performance is invalid. Better criteria is 5- and 10-year periods or, better yet, Rolling Ten Year Periods (1970-1980, 1971-1981, 1972-1982, etc.)

9. REVIEWS DONE INFREQUENTLY

Plan sponsors should review their asset allocation, asset performance, management fees, administrative fees, and employee education programs at least once a year. It doesn't sound like much, but you'd be surprised how few companies do it.

10. PLAN SPONSORS RELY ON CPA'S FOR ADVICE

Only a limited number of CPA's have enough knowledge to provide advice on profit-sharing and 401(k) plans. The main role of a CPA is compliance, and they deal with historical issues in compiling and filing tax forms and performing audits. Most accountants are not in a position to offer insight into plan management. I learned this because I teach CPA's and know dozens of them. Their lack of interest in clients' qualified plans and investment planning is disappointing.

11. PLAN SPONSORS DON'T TAKE ERISA RULE 404(C) SERIOUSLY

While complying with 404(c) doesn't eliminate your plan liability, it can greatly reduce it and make your plan more sound at the same time. The local Bar Association and other legal groups are gearing up for a boom in pension plan liability cases. In the future, attorneys will be on TV soliciting clients who were participants in improperly managed pension plans. If you don't want your workers telephoning one of those attorneys, follow the Four 'C's of 404(c): (choice, change, control and communication).

12. LACK OF WRITTEN INVESTMENT POLICY

This is directly related to No. 11. No pension plan sponsor ever lost a liability case where there was a valid written investment policy in place, even when the plan lost money. Most sponsors with less than $5,000,000 lack an investment policy. It doesn't take much effort to implement a policy (spelling out objectives, diversification, the review process, etc.) and it may provide insight into the direction of your plan.

/s/Kenneth Kaszak
Registered Representative
September 1999

EPILOGUE

The only joy in the
world is to begin.

— Cesare Pavese (Italian writer;1908-1950)

When I was growing up, I was influenced greatly by the movie *From Here to Eternity*. The ingredients for my attraction were the coolness of Montgomery Clift, the toughness of Burt Lancaster, the sexy sweetness of Donna Reed, the swagger of Sinatra, and that intense kiss on the beach.

That movie often made me wonder what it was like to be alive at the time of the Pearl Harbor attack. What was life like in America after the attack? Was the mood of Americans somber or one of anger and retaliation? Did the way people treat each other change as a result?

On September 11, 2001 I came as close to answering those questions as possible. Because I have chosen to be in the investment business, or because it has chosen me, I had to research what was going to happen in the investment markets as a result of the attack and convey my findings to my clients and others.

I prepared a newsletter detailing the experience of the stock markets after national & international events of an adverse nature. I was able to summarize a larger report that studied the movement of the Dow Jones Industrial Average after 28 world events. The report charted the movement of the DJIA after the event unfolded and 4 months later. The study started with the attack of Pearl Harbor, included the start of the Korean War, the Cuban Missile Crisis, the JFK Assassination, the Nixon Resignation, the 1987 stock market plunge and 22 other domestic and world occurrences of an ominous nature.

The median market change after each of the 28 events unfolded was a negative 4.6%. Four months later, the median market change was a positive 12.1% increase.

Stock market movements in the days following September 11th mirrored market history. The DJIA had closed at 9605.50 on September 10th. Trading was halted on September 11th after reports of the attacks in New York and Washington. The markets reopened on Monday September 17th. True to form by the end of trading on Friday the 21st the market had declined to 8235.80. It was a one week decline of 14.25%.

My newsletter was distributed that weekend. I had faith in the research and the numbers but I kept my fingers crossed that the attacks on America weren't the beginning of a series of terrorist attacks that would paralyze the country and depress the psyche of Americans.

Think about how you felt during the weeks after the September attacks. I felt the same way. Like you, I was somber and puzzled and furious all at the same time. Even with those feelings it was my responsibility to keep watch on the capital markets and not react when others without the benefit of my research were making the wrong decision based on emotion.

Much like rock 'n roll the markets didn't forget. They came back. The short-term sellers gave way to the long-term investors. The DJIA increased to 9410.45 by October 11th and to 9608.00 by November 9th. The 14.25% decrease was recaptured in less than two months. Because the percentage gain coming back up has to exceed the percentage loss going down, the increase in less than two months was 16.65%.

As I reread my September 20, 2001 newsletter to my clients in anticipation of writing these pages, I am proud of the words. Those words also provide a crisp memory of how difficult it was to write that newsletter under the circumstances.

Even with the comeback from the 9/11 aftermath the major markets finished with a negative return for the calendar year. The back-to-back losses marked the first time since the inflation-induced '73-'74 debacle that the markets finished with consecutive losses. The negative year in 2001 brought the statistical data to a 52-year Average Annual Return of 13.86%. The number of years in the last 52 that the major market indexes finished with a negative return is now 12.

As we go forward, what does this mean to you?

If you have read this book closely, it doesn't mean much. The AAR of dividend-paying stocks still trounces the returns on bonds and bank instruments and will continue to do so. Inflation is dead. R.I.P. It is so far defeated that the Treasury Department stopped issuing 30-year bonds which had been one of the main revenue raisers for the government since the mid 1970's. Long-term rates now equal short-term rates. The 'inflation premium' that investors required for 25 years has been eliminated due to the efforts of Paul Volcker, Alan Greenspan, Bill Clinton and others.

With the yields on alternative investments remaining low, the dividend-paying stock market is the best place to be. It may not be reflected at any given time due to the behavior of short-minded institutional investors who can move large blocks of stocks in a compressed period of time and cause a price fluctuation up or down. Remember: the short term market is dictated by the behavior of humans who tend to act irrational. Over long periods of time the mechanics of the market will prevail. Buy dividend-paying stocks on a consistent basis. While the institutional investors are attempting to outguess each other, they often drive the price of stocks to a point below the value. Your regular investment program will enable you to buy more shares whose price is only temporarily reduced.

There are at lease two great reasons why the dividend-paying stock markets will be the best place for your long-term money.

The Year 2002 brought with it higher contribution amounts for IRAs, Education IRAs, 401(k) plans and a favorable change in the tax status of Section 529 plans. These increased contribution levels bode well for the stock markets. The majority of the assets going into these types of plans will end up in the stock markets, not the bond markets.

At the time of this writing, there is more money in money market accounts than ever before. That money is going to end up in the stock market or in the purchase of homes, cars, appliances, and other consumer goods. An increase in demand by consumers results in an increase in investment by businesses into plants, equipment, raw materials, research & development, etc.

There were two items that occurred between the time the manuscript for this book was finished and it was prepared for publication. Both items have direct correlation to this book.

When the Enron scandal surfaced, I realized it provided textbook examples of many of the things you learned in this book. It was a classic Price vs. Value story as the price of the stock ran far ahead of the value. That price/value disparity was fed in part of the media who kept adding fuel to the fire by presenting stories about a company whose stock price was increasing rapidly. The media likes such stories. You shouldn't. *For the record, none of my clients owned one share of Enron stock, either directly or through the ownership of stock mutual funds.*

When the Enron bubble broke and the stock price came down to reflect the value, the media gave us story after story about the Enron employees who saw their 401(k) balance tumble from hundreds of thousands of dollars to thousands of dollars. The media thrives equally on stories of quick wealth and the destruction of that wealth. What better real world situation than this one to teach us why we need to own our stocks in mutual funds, that we need to diversify and that many companies have poorly structured 401(k)/Profit-sharing plans?

In my hometown there were two banking stories that give more evidence why banks are the worst place for your money. Mellon Bank sold off its branch banking operations to Citizens Bank. They decided that the business of selling Certificates of Deposit and opening savings accounts and lending money out at 2 percentage points higher was not a growth industry. They are now trying to generate their revenue from fee based business such as their mutual fund entity, Dreyfus Funds.

However, their plan has hit some stumbling blocks. The performance of Dreyfus been less than stellar and some of the officers and directors have been implicated in fraudulent transactions. As a result of their performance, or lack of, and the sale of the retail branches, Dreyfus was dropped as the manager of the State of Pennsylvania's 529 plan.

Across town, PNC, another banking entity that entered the mutual fund business through the acquisition of a high fee, high turnover mutual fund family, had to restate its earnings not once but twice. The restatement brought with it a decline in the share price and the accompanying shareholder lawsuits. Unlike the death of high inflation, the death of Glass-Steagall may have come too soon.

But it is not too soon to end this book. You've learned what you need to know in order to invest your money from this point into the future. You now have the tools to determine which financial information you hear or read is relevant and valid. And you have the tools to detect information that is being used to separate you from your money or not give you fair value in return. These tools should apply to all purchases, not just those connected with the investment business. And you should know how to teach those important items to your family.

It takes a long time to plan, outline, research write, re-write, design, layout and publish a book. Self-doubt and feelings of inadequacy are intermingled with occasional feelings of creativity, accomplishment and illumination. But as the process is winding down for me, I don't want to think of it as an ending. I prefer to think of this final sentence as a beginning.

Ken Kaszak